ONE STATE in ARMS

*A Short Military History
of New Jersey*

by MARK EDWARD LENDER

*TRENTON
NEW JERSEY HISTORICAL COMMISSION, DEPARTMENT OF STATE*

Reprint, 2001, Trenton Printing ◀▦▶ "

New Jersey Historical Commission, Department of State
225 West State Street, P.O. Box 305
Trenton, New Jersey 08625

Designed by Nancy H. Dallaire and Lee R. Parks
Cover designed by Nancy H. Dallaire

Library of Congress Cataloging-In-Publication Data

Lender, Mark Edward, 1947–
    One state in arms: a short military history of New Jersey by Mark Edward
Lender
        p.   cm.—(New Jersey history series: 1)
    Includes bibliographical references.
    ISBN 0-89743-077-8: $9.00
    1. New Jersey—History, Military. I. New Jersey Historical
Commission. II. Title. III. Series.
F134.L5   1991   91-39079
974.9–dc20   CIP

TABLE OF CONTENTS

With love and pride, for
Robert Joseph Lender, U.S.N.

FOREWORD

The last major battle to be fought on New Jersey soil occurred in June of 1780, when British and American forces engaged in a brief, hotly contested campaign around Springfield. New Jersey had been a battleground since 1776, and skirmishing continued there even after the surrender of the British under General Charles Cornwallis, at Yorktown, Virginia, in 1781. As far as the actual shedding of blood was concerned, then, the military history of New Jersey ended with the last shots of the War for Independence. This study, however, looks at the military and New Jersey from the colonial period through the 1980s—a span of almost three centuries. For our purposes, military history therefore is something more than guns and battles. Rather, it encompasses the broad interactions of military affairs—for example, the raising and maintaining of armies, the building of military posts, the economic and social effects of war—with the lives of those who lived in the Garden State. At the same time, we will look as well at the efforts of the sons and daughters of New Jersey who served in the various conflicts that have punctuated American history.

If the scope of this volume is broad, however, the treatment is brief. I have provided only the shortest overview of a vastly larger subject; there is plenty of room for other historians to probe deeper into the state's military past. But slim as it is, my narrative is longer than originally intended—it grew from a treatment planned for some forty pages. Along the way, I found that even a cursory introduction to the subject needed more attention than I had thought.

As the project expanded, I received the encouragement of many friends and helpful critics. At the New Jersey Historical Commission, Mary R. Murrin, Richard Waldron, Howard L. Green and Bernard Bush all read parts of the manuscript and made helpful suggestions for improvement. Outside of the Commission, Professor Stanley N. Worton of Jersey City State College read an early draft of the study with an eye toward making it more useful in the classroom. With similar intent, Barbara Petrick, a careful scholar, provided a searching criticism; her comments led, I hope, to a final version of greater benefit to students and teachers alike. At Kean College of New Jersey, I enjoyed talking over the sections on World War II with James Jandrowitz. Robert Burnett and Sarah Collins of the New Jersey Historical Society were consistently helpful in locating sources and reproducing photographs, and Bob made a number of suggestions on the text itself. On the home front, my wife, Penny Booth Page, gave sections of the manuscript a perceptive reading. I enjoyed her reactions, especially the time she quite literally fell asleep halfway down a page. (I rewrote that page.) To all of the above—many thanks.

I owe a special debt to Mary Murrin at the Historical Commission. She made an art form of friendly badgering when my progress lagged (which was all too frequent), and she served as a supportive critic and careful editor. If *One State In Arms* is any good, much of the credit is hers. If it's no good, forget I mentioned her.

INTRODUCTION

In September 1609, the English explorer Henry Hudson, then sailing under the Dutch flag, made landfall at Sandy Hook. For several days the crew explored ashore, bartering with the native Lenape and recording impressions of the countryside. Before the week ended, however, part of the expedition came to grief. A boat crew sent to investigate Staten Island fell out with an Indian canoe party and, for reasons long forgotten, arrows and shots flew. One John Coleman died in the exchange, and Hudson's men left him in a Sandy Hook grave before heading north to explore the great river that now bears the captain's name. To Coleman we accord the dubious distinction of being the first European combat fatality to be buried in what became New Jersey.

In itself the clash was a minor affair, one of many that marked the initial contacts between Europeans and native Americans. Yet collectively such incidents characterized a good deal of the colonial period: in part, colonization was an act of force, a military exercise from the beginning. (Indeed, as some historians have pointed out, from the Indian perspective it was an outright invasion.) These early conflicts were not the business of formal armies. Rather, the participants were men like Hudson's sailors, fur traders, or parties of colonists who only sometimes had the help of professional military men (such as Miles Standish at Plymouth or John Smith at Jamestown). But the skirmishes were grave matters for the combatants, and some were savage affairs that put the success of colonial ventures in doubt. The 1620s and 1630s saw desperate fighting between the English and the Indians in Virginia and New England; in New Jersey, the Dutch met serious resistance through the 1650s. Of necessity, colonists learned that military concerns were a fact of life.

Americans have been coming to terms with this fact ever since. Martial strife—in whatever form—fear of it, preparations for it, efforts to avoid it, and protests against it, have occupied generations of Americans over more than three centuries of colonial and national history. New Jersey offers a graphic illustration in this regard: since Henry Hudson's clash with the Lenape, at one time or another the state (or colony) has seen frontier struggles, the action of contending armies, and civil strife. When not the host of actual operations, New Jersey has served as a major site for logistics,* supplies, training, and naval ports; it also has been a military research and construction center as well as the scene of active debate over the role of the military in national life and its use as an instrument of policy. In one way or another, the military has left indelible marks on state history.

How military affairs have assumed the prominence they have is the subject of this essay. The focus will be the role of the colony and state of New Jersey in military history from the colonial wars to Vietnam, and will include an overview of operations within New Jersey and of the participation of its citizens in America's far-flung conflicts. Within this broader context, however, there are other concerns. How, for example, have New Jersey residents perceived the role of the military in American life, and how have they dealt with such questions as the military obligations of citizenship? Given the federal government's command and direction of most defense matters, to what extent has an individual state been able to play a distinctive role in military affairs? And of equal importance, how have the citizens of New Jersey reacted over the years as politics and technology have combined to make war a progressively more expensive and deadly business for combatants and noncombatants alike? As these issues played themselves out, some aspects of the state experience emerged as unique. But in general, the history of the military in New Jersey is indicative of the broader sweep of similar developments across the nation—developments of vital importance not only in understanding the past but in facing the future.

*See Glossary, pages 113–118.

CHAPTER ONE

The Early Years:
Arms in the Wilderness

European settlement of New Jersey proceeded with musket*
in hand. The region became an active battleground as colonists
fought not only the Indians, but, as part of the wider affairs
of empire, each other as well. These activities left their mark
on colonial life, and by the late seventeenth century, when
British rule finally brought relative tranquility to the province,
New Jersey already had a considerable martial legacy.

The Dutch were the first whites to establish a foothold in
the region. Almost a decade after Henry Hudson's run-in with
the Indians, Dutch traders and colonial officers began exploring
on two fronts. They pushed up the Delaware to probe the New
Jersey coast, nearby Pennsylvania, and Delaware; in the East,
parties from New Amsterdam on Manhattan Island took initial
steps across the Hudson. The Dutch may have built a
blockhouse on Jersey City Point as early as 1614, but few
colonists considered the area secure from Indian assault. Permanent settlement came only in 1618, when a group from New
Amsterdam took up residence near modern Jersey City. On the
Delaware, Captain Cornelius Mey (for whom Cape May is
named) erected Fort Nassau in 1623 near present Gloucester
City, while other Dutch established themselves in a handful of
fur trading posts scattered along the banks of the river and
Delaware Bay. If the Europeans were ashore, however, they
were hardly welcome.

Most of the Lenape were slow to resist white encroachment.
They were normally a peaceful people, and they generally

9

retreated into the interior after land negotiations with the Dutch. But not all of them went willingly. Tensions between red and white clearly increased during the 1620s, and small-scale incidents took a toll from settlers and Indians alike. Casualties mounted over the next decade, beginning in 1630 when a war party (probably Minquas, not Lenape) killed thirty-two Dutch and destroyed the settlement at Swanendael on Delaware Bay (now the town of Lewes, Delaware). Luckily for the few Dutch on the eastern shore, the Lenape of southern New Jersey avoided confrontations. But fear of all Indians spread and, in the north, the Lenape finally offered determined resistance. The early 1640s saw fighting around Raritan Bay and on Staten Island, culminating in a grisly Dutch massacre of some eighty Lenape near Pavonia in 1643. There was another severe flare-up in the Pavonia area in 1655, and most settlers fled to Manhattan, not to return for another three years. After this, however, armed opposition to the Dutch subsided.

There are no sure figures on the number of Indians in colonial New Jersey. There were probably five to seven thousand in the mid-seventeenth century, and more than that earlier in the century. Whatever the precise number, for several decades the Lenape certainly outnumbered the whites: the combined populations of the Dutch and Swedes (who settled along the Delaware beginning in 1638) was far below one thousand as late as the mid-1660s. Yet Indian numbers ultimately counted for little; all other factors weighed against them. The Europeans employed superior firepower, for instance, as even the cumbersome and inaccurate muskets of the age were effective against traditional Lenape weaponry. More telling was the fact that the white man's diseases had preceded his actual attempts at settlement. Smallpox, influenza, and other maladies decimated the native clans, a situation exacerbated by the acquisition of beverage alcohol from colonists, some of whom encouraged the Indians to drink to excess. These plagues killed more Lenape than combat ever did and so contributed greatly to the European victory. It was a squalid sort of "war," in which the Lenape fought a losing battle against forces they never completely understood.

It fell to the British, who captured New Netherland in 1664, to complete the displacement of the Lenape. British (including New England) immigration to New Jersey increased steadily as the century drew to a close, and the Indians, their numbers thinned through disease, war, and cultural disintegration, could offer no organized opposition. On occasion, rumors of Lenape attacks alarmed colonial villages, and the British were aware that the natives had given the Dutch a hard time. Under the circumstances, noted the colonial historian Samuel Smith, relations with the Indians were "thought good but ticklish."[1] Yet militarily the Lenape were finished; over the early decades of the eighteenth century, most of them left the area in small groups to seek the protection of the Iroquois or to live with tribes in the West. In 1758, in negotiations with colonial officials at Easton, Pennsylvania, the Lenape gave up their remaining claims to New Jersey lands. Some 350 settled on a small tract at Brotherton in Burlington County, while a handful of others remained scattered around the state or assimilated into the European population; the rest left forever. There would still be fears of Indian attack in the province, and some vicious fighting as well; but such threats would come from without. The Lenape were no longer an internal concern.

Even as Europeans skirmished with the Indians, however, they turned on each other. The seventeenth century was an age of imperial rivalries, reflected in New Jersey as the Swedes, Dutch, and British all competed for control of the region. The Dutch exchanged shots on the Delaware River with New England ships and outposts as early as the 1630s and '40s. In 1638, tiny New Sweden established itself in modern Salem and Gloucester counties after reducing Dutch posts there and on the western shore of Delaware Bay. It was a brief victory, for New Sweden was never a prosperous enterprise. In 1655, a Dutch expedition overran the colony—which never numbered more than 400 souls—with a minimum of fighting. In turn, New Netherland never attracted enough immigrants to guarantee its own security. Lodged between hostile British provinces, the Dutch colony lived on borrowed time. In 1664, a British squadron descended upon an almost helpless New Amsterdam and forced a bloodless capitulation of the entire colony, including the territories between the Hudson and the Delaware rivers. A Dutch fleet briefly regained the colony in 1673, but a diplomatic settlement the following year once again confirmed British possession. Thereafter, New Jersey remained securely in the Empire for a century.

These early imperial clashes were not much as far as wars went. There was little serious fighting (although the British did shoot up some of the Dutch posts on the Delaware) and, at least in New Jersey, hardly any enemy population to lord it over. There were probably no more than two hundred Dutch living in the region when it fell to the British. Yet the results were significant: the Empire had acquired an agriculturally rich province and had taken a major step in consolidating its hold in North America. And the fact that final ownership of the region had come through a test of arms was ample notice that the New World—even a relatively small corner of it such as New Jersey—was anything but divorced from the affairs and strife of the Old.

Fighting with the Indians and among the contending European powers helped shape colonial perspectives on military affairs. Significantly, most settlers accepted the fact that they were responsible for their own defense against Indians or other threats. Governments generally involved themselves only in warfare against other governments, hence the martial exchanges between the British and Dutch over New Netherland. They might also, as the Dutch and Swedish authorities did, provide a few troops to accompany colonial ventures, often on the assumption that such men would bring their families and become settlers. These were critical steps in a colony's formative years, when even a handful of trained soldiers could make the difference in the survival of a settlement. On the Delaware in 1644, for example, a Swedish garrison of a dozen men with one cannon turned back a Massachusetts ship probing the area for development by New Englanders. But no European government sent a major armed force to subdue the Indians or to garrison the region; thus, when facing the wilderness, colonists were on their own.

This fact had a number of practical consequences. Early residential patterns, for example, often reflected military necessities. Settlers generally threw up stockades or earthwork fortifications, and a fair number of these saw use against Indians or other Europeans. The town of Bergen, for instance, grew from a stockade erected after the 1655 struggle with the Lenape, and most of the Swedes lived near fortified posts. Even after families established separate homes, housing might still reflect defensive concerns, particularly in isolated areas. The Van

Campen Inn, probably built in 1746 and still standing on its original position overlooking the Delaware in Sussex County, was typical of other structures of the day: its thick stone walls could serve, if necessary, as defensive works. And it *was* necessary: During the 1750s, Indian raids forced settlers from New Jersey and neighboring Pennsylvania to seek refuge within its walls.

Yet most New Jersey settlers, like those elsewhere, lived in simpler quarters and for self-defense had to rely on their personal weapons rather than masonry walls. Even with the removal of the Lenape, colonists feared incursions by tribesmen from across the Delaware River, and it was a rare settler who went unarmed. Indeed, proprietary officials required individuals taking up land grants to own a "good musket" and a six month's supply of powder and shot. Colonists in more settled regions had worries of their own. The colonial government had no

The Van Campen Inn, Sussex County. The house, built about 1746, stands on the Old Mine Road facing the Delaware River. It sheltered local residents when Indian raids threatened from across the river. A fortification stood on the hill behind it during the French and Indian War. PHOTO BY PENNY BOOTH PAGE, COURTESY THE PHOTOGRAPHER.

constabulary* and few court officers; thus residents often looked to themselves to assert rights to land titles or to guard against domestic tumult. In fact, they did so fairly often. From the early 1670s to the 1740s, New Jersey government was frequently unstable; periodic riots broke out over land claims, and more than once civil authority was more apparent than real. It was small wonder that many Jerseymen expected little protection from the colony or from the mother country.

This is not to say that government played no role at all in defense, for there were provisions for it in the basic charters of the colony. The founding proprietors of British New Jersey, John, Lord Berkeley, and Sir George Carteret, saw to this when they promulgated the initial Concessions and Agreement of 1665. The document not only laid the basis for civil government, but also allowed for the creation of a militia, empowered the assembly to levy taxes for supplies and fortifications, named the governor commander of all provincial forces, and allowed him to commission other officers. Colonial governors retained this military role even after royal authority replaced the proprietary government in 1702. And over the years colonial assemblies made various provisions for militia organizations intended to repel threats from without and to quell "all mutinies and rebellions" within.[2]

The colonial militia was rooted in English tradition. Each English county had its military forces, commanded by local officials and intended for regional defense. Parts of this tradition adapted easily to the American context; most northern colonies based militia companies in individual townships, and southern colonies used counties as military districts. New Jersey, like most other colonies, also assumed that all able-bodied men should serve, and militia laws—which changed little over the late seventeenth and early eighteenth centuries—called for the periodic drill of all free men between the ages of sixteen and fifty. In times of need, the government could call up militiamen by lot for short tours of duty. The enrolling of all able-bodied men was a legal recognition of the fact that colonials had to bear the burdens of regional defense themselves. Gradually, partly from English heritage and partly from the realities of life in the wilderness, colonials accepted the notion that bearing arms in the common defense was an obligation one owed the community.

Some colonies, especially those with frontiers exposed to Indian or foreign attack, maintained relatively effective militia organizations. Units trained regularly, governments enforced enrollment laws, and there was a modicum of discipline. In New Jersey, however, the frontier passed sooner than in other British provinces, and most citizens felt little need to keep the militia up to snuff. Indeed, while it existed on paper, the local military was a rusty sword: enforcement of militia law was lax, drills were infrequent, and few residents considered the militia a reliable force. During the land riots of the 1740s, for example, which occasionally bordered on civil war and easily qualified as "rebellion," control over the militia was so feeble that Governor Jonathan Belcher made no attempt to call it out against the rioters.

Nor did all Jerseymen agree with the terms of militia service. In West New Jersey, pacifist Quakers, who were a majority of the population there, took particular exception to the universal enrollment provisions. Refusing to bear arms left them subject to arrest and fines, and the Quakers wanted legal exemption from duty. Their representatives in the assembly made repeated efforts toward this end, but at various times political opponents proved too strong or exemption measures that were passed in the assembly died in the governor's council. The issue remained a matter of debate throughout the colonial period, and the running dispute proved one more impediment to the creation of a reliable local military. In fact, no colonial governor of New Jersey ever forged an effective fighting force from the formal militia structure.

Yet the quality of the militia was only part of the story. Ineffectual or not, the mere existence of a militia was significant. At least as it evolved in the early eighteenth century, the militia provided the semblance of a colonywide military system and was one more sign that the colony was maturing. The scattered pre-British settlements could not have supported even the pretense of such a system. The militia was also popularly based, and as the colony grew its heritage was one of local residents in arms— not a reliance on troops from the mother country.

Finally, there was a grimmer reality just below the surface of even a weak militia: a township militia company (or part of it), particularly in a remote area such as Sussex County, could respond to a crisis faster than the forces of any central government. This was critical, for, as historian John Ferling has pointed out, colonials were resigned to the fact that local residents and their homes were military targets. Frontier war was a messy business whether attacks came from Indians or, as they did in some colonies, from the French. There were no "rules" of war on the European model that might act to spare noncombatants, women, and children. The lesson of Swanendael and Pavonia and of individual incidents and skirmishes was that when the shooting started, anyone could become a casualty. There were bitter reminders of this fact when Indian raids from across the Delaware fell on isolated New Jersey farms. If residents did not organize to protect themselves, no one was going to do it for them.

The stakes were high when action threatened: colonists on the firing line or in the path of a raid stood to lose family, life, and livelihood. It was an early version of "total war," in which distinctions between "military" and "nonmilitary" targets blurred. Those who stood to lose all—or feared that they might—worried little about the niceties of who among the enemy died; thus at Pavonia in 1643 the Dutch slaughtered women and children along with the men. Had they possessed the strength, the Swedes would have done the same to the unoffending Lenape on the Delaware. "Nothing would be better," wrote New Sweden's governor, Johan Printz, "than that a couple of hundred soldiers should be sent here and kept here until we broke the necks of all of them."[3] Real security, most settlers believed, came only with the elimination of an enemy, not an Old World–style peace treaty that might leave the foe intact. The final departure of the Lenape is worth noting in this regard: aside from opening new lands for settlement, the exodus removed the last possibility of an Indian threat to New Jersey's internal security. Men responsible for their own defense did not relish having to fight the same opponent twice; it was better to eliminate them, one way or another, once and for all. Such feelings may have been less pronounced in New Jersey than in colonies facing more powerful Indian opponents, but Jerseymen shared some of these sentiments. It was an outlook that led people to expect the worst from war and to strip away most of the romantic trappings still attached to "the sport of kings" in Europe. It also led to the conviction that, if they had to wage war at all, they had best wage a very hard brand of it. These were conclusions derived from experience, and they were not forgotten as new military crises loomed on the horizon.

New Jersey in the Empire: The French and Indian Wars

New Jersey flourished under British rule. West New Jersey became a largely Quaker commonwealth when William Penn gained control of Lord Berkeley's proprietary interests in the mid-1670s. In the East, the population was more varied and wont to quarrel bitterly over conflicting land titles. But immigrants came to both sections, and when the provinces merged and became a single royal colony in 1702 the population stood at about 15,000, a figure which increased fourfold by midcentury. They were not an easy people to govern, and proprietary and royal governors often had a hard time controlling the disputatious assemblies. But representative government took firm root, as did the organs of justice. Land titles were a perpetual bone of contention—and sometimes a source of riot— as groups of settlers and investors (notably the East Jersey Board of Proprietors) argued over the rights to valuable tracts of real estate.

As the arguments proceeded, so did agriculture; with the exception of a few bad years, crops were good and the province was well on its way to its later reputation as the "Garden State." Manufactures were extremely limited, but there was important activity in charcoal making, iron smelting, and milling in support of agriculture. And while direct trade with the rest of the world was slight, New Jersey produce found ready markets in neighboring New York and Philadelphia. For the small colony, membership in the empire was paying handsome dividends.

The empire, however, received its due. As New Jersey matured as a colony, the imperial rivalry for North America intensified, and this time the enemy was the most dangerous of all—France. New France extended from the Gulf of St. Lawrence to the Great Lakes, and by 1718 it had reached through the Ohio and Mississippi River valleys to New Orleans. Indian alliances strengthened its military capabilities, and by the mid-1700s New France was poised to cut the British colonies off from the Transappalachian West and to threaten the security

of the entire frontier. Fearing encirclement, the colonists repeatedly followed the mother country to war. Between 1689 and
1763, they joined in four declared wars against the French and
took part in a series of frontier actions that erupted in periods
of technical "peace." In the early 1740s, colonial troops also
fought in the Caribbean when Britain and Spain waged a costly
war for possessions there. These contests were often brutal
affairs, and the toll in blood and treasure was high.

New Jersey never became a major battleground during these
conflicts, removed as it was from Canada and the western
frontiers. But the province provided men and money, and,
relative to its size, made significant contributions to the various
war efforts.

Initial attempts to fight beyond the borders of the province,
however, were exercises in frustration. During Queen Anne's
War (1702–13), New Jersey raised several hundred men and
£8,000 in support of British-led expeditions against both Port
Royal in Nova Scotia and Montreal. Port Royal fell, but the
move on Montreal got no further than Albany, where it fizzled
for lack of logistical support. Fighting flared again in 1739, this
time against Spain in the War of Jenkins' Ear. It was disastrous:
British and colonial troops—including an unknown number of
Jerseymen—were butchered in a bungled assault on Cartagena
(in what is now Colombia). Things improved only marginally
when this conflict blended into a wider war against France (King
George's War, 1744–48). In 1745, a New England expedition
captured the French stronghold of Louisburg, which commanded the Gulf of St. Lawrence. In an effort to exploit this
victory, the New Jersey Assembly voted £10,000 and some 660
troops; once more the intention was to send these men against
Montreal. Yet the British again failed to provide the necessary
supplies and the attack never got rolling. Worse, the Jerseymen
threatened to mutiny when their pay was late; they remained
in ranks only because their commander, Colonel Philip Schuyler,
paid them out of his own pocket, after which their units disbanded late in 1747. When the war ended inconclusively the
following year—the treaty even returned Louisburg to the
French—the colonies, New Jersey included, saw little reason to
rejoice.

Despite the gloom surrounding these events, some significant
points emerged. Perhaps the most instructive was the way in

which New Jersey chose to fight: evidently, there was little thought of sending the militia to fight a long war far from home. Like most other colonies, the province decided early on that committing militia to lengthy campaigning against a strong enemy was impractical. It would have been politically unpopular, weakened local defense, and disrupted regional agriculture; worse, sending the local troops against the well-trained French and their Indian allies would have been an invitation to murderous casualties. No militia unit fought in any of these conflicts. Serious warfare, colonials generally agreed, required volunteers under regular leadership and discipline. Thus the men who marched to Albany or sailed to Port Royal and Cartagena were long-term volunteers organized in special colonial regiments or serving directly in British outfits. Their service established a military precedent: New Jersey would raise men like them whenever similar circumstances arose, while maintaining the militia for short-term duties close to home.

These New Jersey regulars saw considerable action over the next decades, for the peace that ended King George's War was really only a truce. Both sides began sparring for a showdown in the early 1750s, and there was major fighting (including the ghastly defeat of British General Edward Braddock's column in western Pennsylvania in 1754) before Britain formally declared war in 1755. Variously known as the Seven Years' War, the French and Indian War, or the Great War for Empire, the conflict was monumental; fighting raged wherever Britain and her enemies had conflicting interests, which ranged from the New World to Europe and on to India. New Jersey's participation reflected the magnitude of the struggle. Over the course of the war, the assembly contributed some £204,000, which, on a per capita basis, was the fourth largest financial effort of any of the British colonies. Thomas Purvis, a careful historian, has estimated that three thousand New Jersey soldiers served as regulars in British or provincial units before the war ended in 1763. If so, it was a "level of participation requiring the enlistment of every fourth free male between the ages of sixteen and forty-five who was not a Quaker."[4] Whatever the precise figures, this was easily the biggest military effort in provincial history.

The men who enlisted in the provincial regiment—known as the "Jersey Blues"—compiled a proud but tragic record. In 1756, after guard duty in Sussex County, 500 of the New Jersey regulars under Colonel Peter Schuyler joined British forces in upper New York and ultimately marched to the post at Oswego. It was not an auspicious campaign: in August 1757, the French routed the garrison and captured Schuyler and half of the regiment. Those who escaped fared little better. Sent to Fort William Henry on Lake George, they were ambushed and mauled in July 1758 along with some New York provincials. After the battle, a French priest recalled seeing some Ottawa Indians eating the roasted flesh of one of the prisoners. The next month, more Jersey Blues fell captive or died when the French took Fort William Henry itself. Colonial hatred of the French and Indians reached new heights, while the prowess of British arms became suspect among many provincials.

Despite these disasters, New Jersey made good its losses by enlisting new recruits. Before the final defeat of France the Jersey Blues saw tough duty at Fort Niagara, Fort Ticonderoga, and, when the Spanish came in on the side of France, at Havana, Cuba, which a British-colonial force took in 1762. The Jersey Blues emerged as one of the most distinguished colonial regiments, and in the following decade some of the young men who gained experience in its ranks would make themselves useful to New Jersey outfits in the Continental Army.

While the Jersey Blues fought their battles far from home, local combatants waged the war on native soil; unlike the other campaigns against the French, the Seven Years' War spilled into New Jersey. Indian raids were a threat along the Delaware River frontier, and after the declaration of war, four hundred northern New Jersey militia rallied to the defense of eastern Pennsylvania, which already had experienced attacks. This group saw no combat before dispersing, but the show of force, plus negotiations with the tribes, temporarily forestalled hostilities. But the peace collapsed in mid-1757. In the following year, twenty-seven Sussex County residents, most of them farmers and their families, died in the fighting. The Treaty of Easton, which settled Indian claims to New Jersey lands, also put a stop to the raids, but the colony remained jittery. The assembly made provision for a series of blockhouses along the Delaware and garrisoned the area with a patrol force of over two hundred rangers. Memories of the incidents died hard, as Sussex County "old timers" were around to relate stories of the Indian fighting as late as the 1840s.

The noncombatant "home front" was active as well. New Jersey farmers did a brisk business in produce with the royal and provincial forces, and contractors did well hauling military supplies, firewood, furniture, and other necessities. They also built barracks. British army troops were in the province frequently during the conflict for staging, rest, and resupply. As a consequence, the assembly voted support for barracks in 1758, after the populace complained of the inconveniences inherent in lodging soldiers in private homes and public buildings, which they were required to do under the English Mutiny Act of 1756. Contractors built quarters to hold three hundred men each in Perth Amboy, Elizabethtown, New Brunswick, Burlington, and Trenton—the last of which stand today. For several years these

The Old Barracks, Trenton. The colonial government built the barracks in 1758 to house British and provincial troops during the French and Indian War. Similar barracks stood in Perth Amboy, New Brunswick, Princeton, and Bordentown; the soldiers they housed became an important part of local society, often taking part-time jobs when off duty and spending their pay with town merchants. The construction of the barracks also made it unnecessary for the colonial and British governments to quarter troops on the civilian population. PHOTO BY NANCY H. DALLAIRE, COURTESY THE PHOTOGRAPHER.

were garrison towns, and local shopkeepers, taverners, and other merchants had the benefit of the soldiers' business. If the protests against quartering the troops on the populace were eloquent, there is no record of complaint about the redcoats spending money locally. In fact, New Jersey residents generally adjusted quite well to the army in their midst.

The peace of 1763 was decisive. It drove the French from North America and brought new power and prestige to the empire. New Jersey rejoiced at the victory, proud to have fought the common enemy. Yet the war had serious consequences for New Jersey, many of which were not immediately apparent. Politically, the colony would never be the same. In raising men, money, and supplies, in cooperating with royal officials, and in the myriad other administrative tasks that go along with a major military venture, colonial leaders learned a great deal about themselves: they had the skills necessary to run a government and fight a war. There were mistakes—there always are—and supplies were wasted and certain funds poorly expended. But the New Jersey troops received a reasonable measure of financial and logistical support; certainly they were better off than the men who had threatened mutiny for want of pay in King George's War. The Seven Years' War, whatever else it was, served as a test of local leadership. In their own way, the local assembly leaders and other colonial functionaries who managed the civilian side of the war also emerged as "veterans." It is difficult to tell such men—as the Crown later tried to do—that they were not capable of governing themselves.

War finance was a case in point. Since the 1709 campaign against the French, New Jersey had emitted bills of credit— paper money—to pay for military expenses. The British, who were adamantly opposed to colonies issuing their own currencies, never approved the practice; they preferred that the provincial assemblies levy taxes to pay obligations. The British could, and did, make a good case for their position on strictly fiscal grounds; but they missed the political point. New Jersey, like other colonies facing similar circumstances, had its economic arguments as well, also good ones. The central issue, however, was that the assembly considered itself capable of handling its own monetary and tax questions and saw British interference in such matters as unwarranted. Even as loyal subjects of King George they chafed at such treatment. If few saw the controversy as one of dire import in 1763, it was largely over such issues that, in large part, the empire came to grief in 1775.

CHAPTER TWO

The War For Independence

In April 1775, when Massachusetts farmers were trading shots with the king's regulars at Lexington and Concord, New Jersey was not a hotbed of revolution. The colony nursed its grievances against the Crown, but feelings were less intense than in New England and Virginia. Royal Governor William Franklin preferred accommodation to confrontation and remained fairly popular even as rebellion loomed elsewhere. New Jersey had sent delegates to the Continental congresses, but they, as well as other local patriots, had adopted a cautious posture. Theirs was a small province which could do little in the dispute with the mother country without the help of the larger colonies, especially its neighbors, Pennsylvania and New York. Nevertheless, when the call to arms came, hesitation gave way to action and a war effort that lasted until the peace treaty of 1783. During that time, the colony probably saw more fighting than any other (a situation with a certain irony, given New Jersey's lack of early militancy).

In October 1775, faced with an enemy army besieged in Boston and the prospect of major war, the Continental Congress resolved to field a regular Continental army. It called on New Jersey to raise two of the new regiments, each with 728 men of all ranks, and the Provincial Congress quickly complied. Patriot spirits were high, and volunteers quickly filled the ranks.

Recruits were to serve for a year and bring their own weapons in return for $5 a month and a clothing issue. By January 1776, the New Jersey Continentals were reporting for duty around New York, and in February a third state regiment joined them. Sent north to reinforce American units that had invaded Canada the year before, the First and Second New Jersey headed toward Quebec; patriot commanders, however, diverted the Third to the Mohawk River Valley in western New York. Morale was high. Far from home, the Jerseymen greeted the Declaration of Independence with cheers in July, and one young captain prayed that his men would "acquit themselves like soldiers . . . & return crowned with wreaths of unfading *Laurels.*"[1]

But there was no glory. The British counterattacked near Quebec, and the First and Second New Jersey took serious casualties as the rebel army fell back. During the retreat, they suffered from the ravages of a smallpox epidemic, and by July 1776 they had pulled all the way back to Fort Ticonderoga in New York State. The Third regiment, which had held the Mohawk Valley against the Indians and tories, joined them there to await an expected British assault. The retreat had staggered patriot morale, and the knowledge that the enemy was coming south during the fall did little to restore confidence. Then, in November and December, news of the invasion of New Jersey and General George Washington's retreat across the Delaware virtually destroyed any remaining determination to fight. The majority of the New Jersey troops just wanted to go home and look after their families. Ignoring pleas from Continental General John Sullivan that they stay on in the north, units of the First and Second marched south as their enlistments expired near the end of the year; the Third followed them home and disbanded as well before March of 1777. New Jersey's first Continental regiments were gone.

While the Continentals were learning the realities of war, New Jersey's militia were also undergoing a baptism by fire. Local patriots had taken over the militia by mid-1775, having purged it of officers loyal to Governor Franklin, and they did their best to supply and train its units. In the new militia, which had evolved directly from the colonial militia, every man between sixteen and fifty was to enroll for duty in a township company. Each company elected its own junior officers, while senior commanders received commissions from the Provincial

Congress (or, after independence, from the state government). Philemon Dickinson and William Livingston were the first militia generals, and while Dickinson developed into a fine officer, Livingston saw duty only briefly before the state chose him to serve as governor. In 1775 and 1776, the New Jersey militia played an active role in regional patriot military operations, assisting in rounding up tories, collecting supplies, and cooperating with General Washington as he prepared for the defense of New York City.

Enthusiasm, however, was no substitute for training and experience. With the rest of the patriot army, the militia were driven out of New York in September, and in the following weeks most of them retreated into their home state. The respite was only brief, as in late November a British column under Charles, Lord Cornwallis, climbed the palisades and overran Fort Lee (on the site of the present city of the same name). It was a stinging defeat. Thoroughly disheartened, the militia often melted away as Cornwallis followed up his success. Unable to regroup for a stand, and outraged at what he considered disgraceful conduct on the part of the militia, Washington withdrew across New Jersey and crossed the Delaware into Pennsylvania in early December. For New Jersey, this was the darkest hour. Although militia units remained active in the southern and northern sections of the state, and many men later returned to the colors after the rebel successes at Trenton and Princeton, the "Spirit of '76" was exhausted.

In retrospect, it is easy to see that the citizen-soldiers could not have matched the enemy regulars. Even without the catastrophes of 1776, the state faced too many impediments to its efforts to create a battleworthy militia. The militia law was never strong enough to compel the participation of all eligible men, and tours of duty (usually only weeks at a time) for those who did turn out were too short to allow adequate training or lengthy operations. Moreover, New Jersey's manpower resources were too limited to allow fighting a major war with militia. Of the state's nearly 140,000 people, perhaps some 27,000 were men of military age. But of these, about 20 percent—around 5,000 men—were Quaker pacifists, while another 3,200 or so were lost to the loyalists. Certain elected officials and other civilians in trades considered vital to the war effort received exemptions, while thousands more served at sea as

privateers.* In all, at least 11,200 men, over 40 percent of those
of military age, were unavailable for militia duty. There were
even problems with militia willing to fight. As a rule, they
preferred staying close to home, fearing the worst for families
left unprotected against enemy raids. In many parts of New
Jersey these were legitimate concerns, and even Washington
occasionally admitted as much. Fortunately, the militia did its
best work locally. As the war dragged on, militiamen became
adept at harassing British patrols, gathering intelligence,
performing routine garrison duty, and serving as a local constabulary. They also performed a crucial political function,
surviving as a constant line of defense against counterrevolution.
With militia on the scene, local tories never had a chance to
organize effectively. A loyalist might become active politically
or militarily, but only at the risk of becoming the target of a
rebel neighbor. The militia, no matter how ineffective in organized battle, provided the muscle the state government
needed to win the political war against the king.

Rather than place its military hopes in the militia, New Jersey
agreed with General Washington on the need for long-term,
properly trained and equipped regular soldiers. From time to
time, the province raised "State Troops"—long-term units
enlisted to hold key positions or provide specialized services,
such as artillery* duty, that militia could not provide. Over the
course of the war, some of these units served with distinction,
especially state artillery units, which performed as integral parts
of the Continental Army.

For the most part, however, New Jersey patriots pinned their
hopes on a reorganized Continental Army. This new force
would replace the Continentals who had fought during the 1776
campaign and reached the end of their enlistments in late 1776
and early 1777. It would be organized and trained to fight on
the European model* as Washington wished; after 1777 American regulars would face British regulars. This approach was
hardly novel; colonial New Jersey had come to the same decision on how to fight during the French and Indian War, when
the result was the raising of the "Jersey Blues." Regular battalions (a term used interchangeably with *regiments*) would re-
move the heaviest combat burden from the local militia, which
could then concentrate on regional security matters. This ar-
rangement also would leave the citizen-soldiers in a position

to work their farms and keep the state's economy functioning. Congress voted the authority for the new regiments (the "Second Establishment") in September 1776, although recruiting did not begin in earnest until early 1777. Regulations called for enlistments of three years or for the duration of the war, with recruits receiving bounties of $20 and a yearly clothing issue. Men who served for the duration also would receive 100 acres of land after discharge.

New Jersey raised four regiments for the new Continental Line. They usually served together as the New Jersey Brigade, often with another outfit attached. This additional unit was "Spencer's Regiment," raised directly under Congressional authority and named after its colonel, Oliver Spencer of New Jersey. So many of its personnel were from New Jersey that it was unofficially called the Fifth New Jersey. Brigade command went to William Maxwell of Sussex County. Maxwell— "Scotch Willie" to his troops—had a solid record in the French and Indian War, and along with William Alexander (Lord Stirling) received a colonelcy in one of the original New Jersey Continental battalions of 1775. When Alexander left to serve as a major general under Washington, Maxwell became the ranking Jerseyman and got a brigadier's star in late 1776. Never a brilliant leader, he was dependable and willing to fight. He served until 1780, when he resigned, pleading ill health. The brigade then passed to Colonel Elias Dayton. Dayton also had fought the French, as a junior officer in the Jersey Blues, and he had led the old Third New Jersey in 1776. Early in the war he had hoped for a reconciliation with the Crown, but after independence he was a loyal and genuinely gallant combat leader. He gained the esteem of Washington, who had him promoted to brigadier general in 1783.

Recruiting the new regiments was a constant trial for the state. The enthusiasm of 1775 had evaporated in the wake of the early defeats, and most of the veterans of 1775 and 1776 chose not to reenlist. Moreover, men with farms and families saw little reason to leave home for years of Continental duty when they could serve instead on short local militia tours. Tacitly, New Jersey, like the other states, admitted that it could not attract to the ranks large numbers of yeoman farmers— those who composed the property-holding middle-class backbone of society. Instead, recruiters settled for any able-bodied and effective volunteers they could get, which meant enlisting indentured servants, the young, the poor, free blacks, and even a few Indians and slaves. Many were drifters who left no trace in the towns from which they enlisted. Of the New Jersey Continentals with verifiable backgrounds, most (probably some 80 percent) came from the poorest two-thirds of society. About 57 percent were landless. Thus the New Jersey regulars left relatively little behind them when they joined the army.

Even with these enlistments, manpower remained a chronic problem. Desertion ran as high as 40 percent in 1777; while this figure fell to 10 percent by 1779, these were still serious losses. At times, New Jersey recruiters were so desperate that they took petty criminals and tories into the ranks—the latter joining to avoid trials for treason. In 1778 and 1780, acute troop shortages forced the state to draft militiamen for nine-month tours in the Continental Line. These measures produced enough soldiers to keep the regiments in the field, but only at reduced strength. In 1779, Congress reduced the state's contribution to three battalions, and then to two in 1781. In 1778, when there were more state Continentals than ever, New Jersey Brigade muster rolls carried some 1,600 officers and men; by 1783 there were fewer than 700. Like the units of the other states, New Jersey's were thin battalions.

There were other New Jersey troops in the field, however, and they served in units now almost forgotten. As revolutionary government took hold, thousands of state residents remained loyal to the king. Many of them fled from patriot lines, harassed and in fear for their lives, and with their homes and farms confiscated by patriot authorities. Great numbers of these "refugees," as they came to be called, had lost all but life itself, and, striking out of bases in British-occupied New York, they fought desperately in the tory cause. While precise numbers are not known, several thousand took part in raids under the auspices of the Board of Associated Loyalists, headed by the former royal governor, William Franklin. Others enlisted as regular troops with the British or in the "Green Coats" (after their uniforms) of General Cortlandt Skinner, New Jersey's last attorney general under royal government. At the height of its strength, Skinner's brigade included five regiments, and they developed a well-earned reputation for toughness. They fought throughout the war on far-flung fields; many died hundreds of miles from their native province during British-led operations in the South. After the war, the remnants of these outfits, along with Franklin's irregulars, generally went into permanent exile in Britain and Canada.

Battleground: A State at War

As New Jersey struggled to keep its troops in the field, the tides of war swept the state with deadly regularity. The British invasion of 1776 demoralized patriots and elated the tories: the British commander, General William Howe, was confident that he had subdued the province. At one point, hundreds of New Jersey rebels were coming in each day to accept a royal pardon. The fact that Howe had not finished off the Continental Army caused little concern; he planned on mopping up any remnants of Washington's command in the spring of 1777, if they had not dissolved of their own accord. In the meantime, he deployed his redcoats for the winter in a chain of posts across the center of the state from Perth Amboy to Bordentown. General Howe could be excused for thinking that total victory was within his grasp.

It nearly was, and no one knew it better than George Washington. His Continentals, their numbers dwindling, were temporarily safe in Pennsylvania, having brought all available boats over with them in order to prevent Howe's pursuit. But time was running out for the cause, and Washington decided to risk virtually everything on a desperate counterattack. The plan called for three rebel columns to cross the Delaware on Christmas night and strike the British post at Trenton. The garrison there were Hessians, German mercenaries in British hire, and under the command of Colonel Johann Rall.

The operation went wrong from the start: the weather was bad and the river was ice-choked. Only the column under Washington's personal command crossed on time. Electing to play out the game, the patriot chief mounted the attack alone. Legend has it that the Hessians were so busy celebrating Christmas that they neglected to post an adequate guard. This was not the case. Rall's security was not worse than usual, but Washington's twelve-mile march from the north of town went undetected and the rebels surged into the dark streets of Trenton almost unopposed. The stunned Hessians never were able to rally. The battle lasted under an hour, and at the cost of five patriot casualties (two of whom froze to death) Washington killed some thirty of the enemy and took over nine hundred prisoners; about six hundred Hessians got away. It was not much as far as battles went, but the dramatic effect was terrific. Sagging patriot morale was galvanized, and a shocked General Howe was forced to react.

Washington moved back into Trenton on December 31, and on New Year's Day his units fought a tough delaying action as the British advanced on the town (a running fight now called the second battle of Trenton). The enemy field commander was again Cornwallis, and at day's end he seemingly had the Americans pinned against the Delaware; he would, he told a subordinate, "bag the fox" in the morning. In not attacking immediately that evening, Cornwallis committed one of the great blunders of the war. That night, Washington left his campfires burning and slipped out of Trenton on an unguarded road. The next morning, he mauled several British regiments at Princeton, and only exhaustion stopped his men from sweeping into thinly held New Brunswick and capturing the British pay chest. Instead, by January 7 he had led his troops to the safety of winter quarters at Morristown. Without question, Washington's "Christmas Campaign"—the battles at Trenton and Princeton—must stand as one of the stellar feats of American arms. His victories had done nothing less than save the Revolution.

The stay at Morristown was critical for the army. Morris County was secure patriot country—local militia, while scared, had stood by their guns during the darkest days of 1776—and the hilly terrain was defensible. Washington used the winter to rebuild Continental ranks while sending an almost constant series of raids against the British, who then held only a narrow strip of territory between Perth Amboy and New Brunswick. General Howe never felt strong enough to strike north, and with the return of spring the new patriot army was ready to fight. The Crown had lost forever the chance to catch Washington while he was preoccupied with a complete reorganization of his regular battalions.

Morristown itself changed that winter, and its story reflected much of what civilian New Jersey endured throughout the conflict. A quiet hamlet of some 250 souls before the war, it was transformed by the coming of the army into the military capital of the Revolution. The Continentals used the locale as a training, staging, and logistical center; at various times it also served as a major winter encampment. The winter of 1779–80 was the most terrible of the war: snows were enormous, the cold bitter, and supplies so short that Washington was forced to impress* food from local farmers to keep the army from dissolving. The town found its new fame a mixed blessing. When the army had money, which was not often later in the war, the market for local crops, stock, and products was good. But after 1777, a ruinous inflation brought this early prosperity to an abrupt halt. The patriot government had run out of money, and in order to finance the war effort, Congress and the states flooded the market with millions of dollars in paper bills. This proved disastrous for farmers, who saw crops sold—or im-pressed—for depreciated currency or almost worthless promissory notes. Morristown also lost heavily to outbreaks of smallpox and other maladies that traveled with the army. The village learned, as others would learn, that there was a very thin line between the fighting front and the home front.

When the campaign of 1777 opened, New Jersey already had earned its place as the "cockpit of the Revolution." The next several years, however, would see fighting on a scale far beyond that of 1776. In June 1777, after failing to lure Washington into a showdown fight, Howe quit New Jersey. Taking ship in New York, by September he had sailed up Chesapeake Bay and launched an invasion that drove the Americans out of Philadelphia. Major battles at Brandywine, Germantown, and at forts Mifflin and Mercer (the latter was on the New Jersey side of the Delaware River below Philadelphia) proved that the Continentals were game and tough opponents; but in the end Washington retired to winter quarters at Valley Forge.

Like the rest of the Continental Line, the New Jersey Brigade had learned a great deal through bitter experience. Maxwell's men had fought well at Brandywine and Germantown, and at Valley Forge they sharpened their skills under the drill of General Friedreich, Baron von Steuben, a former aide to Frederick the Great of Prussia. Steuben trained the American regulars to fight on the European model, and the arrival of generous shipments of French arms and supplies assured the rebels of adequate equipment for the coming campaign. The

Valley Forge winter encampment was cruel, but the army that emerged in 1778 was better prepared than ever to carry the war to the enemy.

On June 18, 1778, the armies clashed again at the Battle of Monmouth. Changing British strategy led to the engagement: With French entry into the war, the British evacuated Philadelphia in order to meet military commitments on other fronts. General Henry Clinton, who had replaced Howe, sent many of his men back to New York by ship, along with Pennsylvania tories afraid to stay behind. But Clinton marched some 10,000 of his best men across New Jersey, and Washington caught him at Monmouth Courthouse, near Freehold. It was the longest single day's fighting of the war, and the improvements in the Continental Line were apparent. After rebel outfits under General Charles Lee, the ranking Continental officer behind Washington, retreated before British pressure—which ultimately led to Lee's court martial and dismissal from command—the line stabilized under Washington's personal leadership. For the rest of the day, the Continentals traded volley for volley with the best the enemy could throw against them. The opponents had fought one another to a standstill when darkness ended the exchange, and Clinton then slipped away in the night, getting his men back to New York. Yet the patriots were elated; their army had never looked better, and even British officers voiced a grudging respect for the Continental performance. The Continental Army had come of age.

The Monmouth campaign also revealed a New Jersey radically different from the province of 1776. This time, the British advance through the state did not spread panic. The militia fought well alongside the regulars; if the local forces still did not turn out in sufficient numbers to please patriot leaders, at least there was no repetition of the disgrace of 1776. Civilians moved livestock out of harm's way, gave what help they could to patriot troops, or kept their heads down as the fighting raged, but very few fled before the redcoats. None came in to take a king's pardon, and there was no revival of tory activity as Clinton's men moved east; for the royal troops, New Jersey clearly was enemy territory.

This war-wise New Jersey conduct was born of bitter lessons learned since 1776. Patriot government was firmly established, but large parts of the state (especially those near New York

Molly Pitcher at the Battle of Monmouth. *The story of Molly Pitcher at Monmouth became part of the folklore of the War for Independence. She was actually Mary Hays, a cannoneer's wife who brought water to the thirsty gunners. The battle lasted all day and was fought in temperatures above ninety degrees. The guns, cleaned between rounds, also needed water. Most of the women who saw combat were the wives or relatives of soldiers and served, as Mary Hays did, in support of the combat troops.* COURTESY THE NEW JERSEY HISTORICAL SOCIETY.

City) were exposed to British and tory raids, and no amount of patriot vigilance could guarantee complete security. At various times, sections of Bergen and Monmouth counties were a virtual no-man's-land as patriot militia and regulars skirmished with redcoats and tories. Coastal and river areas swarmed with rebel privateers, whose activities invited a series of British reprisals. As the years wore on, both sides committed atrocities, and bitterness between the contending forces deepened. This was particularly the case in actions pitting loyalists against former patriot neighbors; civil wars are seldom pleasant. Farmers knew all too much about having crops and stock stolen or expropriated by the enemy, and sometimes by American soldiers. People endured without enthusiasm, and many were grim; but in war it is endurance which in the end brings victory.

After 1778 the war moved to the South. Except for a vicious clash at Springfield, New Jersey, in 1780, Monmouth ended the major fighting in the North. For the New Jersey Continentals, however, the contest was as active as ever. Their final year of campaigning—1781—was one of paradox; it started in disgrace but ended in glory. Camped at Pompton in January, the Jersey Brigade followed the Pennsylvania Line into mutiny when they could no longer suffer the trials of poor supply, late pay, and winter cold. But the numerous Pennsylvanians were able to negotiate a largely favorable settlement of their grievances, whereas the New Jersey revolt was weak enough for Washington to crush with New England troops. Two ringleaders were summarily shot as a warning against further trouble.

Yet the brigade was still a fighting unit, and it redeemed itself soon enough. A group of picked men marched south with the Marquis de Lafayette in February to counter an incursion into Virginia led by the turncoat Benedict Arnold. Commanded by Lieutenant Colonel Francis Barber, who had been an Elizabethtown schoolmaster before the war and was probably New Jersey's most dashing combat leader, these troops served with distinction. In September, the rest of the New Jersey Line also moved into Virginia as part of the operation that trapped Washington's old opponent, Lord Cornwallis, at Yorktown. The brigade took an active part in combat operations during the siege, and was present on October 19 when the redcoats stacked their arms while their band, tradition says, played a popular tune called "The World Turned Upside Down." With victory won, the troops returned to quarters around New York City, there to await the peace of 1783 and be discharged after long and distinguished service.

CHAPTER THREE

An Uneasy Peace

The War for Independence had a profound impact on American military history. To those who came of age during and after the struggle, it seemed that a citizen-soldiery—the freemen in arms—had brought a European professional army low, which to a great extent was true. The glow of victory, however, tended to exalt this idealized view of rebel arms, expecially the role of the militia, while obscuring less pleasant aspects of the recent past. The deprivations of the Continentals, erratic militia performance, and the fact that many Americans had avoided service altogether faded from public consciousness. A soldiery of free citizens embodied as militia seemed synonymous with liberty, while professional troops recalled the tyranny of Europe. This view was so widespread that even the fact that patriots had raised a regular army themselves received short shrift; indeed, when Congress sent the Continental Line home, it did so not with thanks but with a lecture on the dangers of maintaining a standing army in time of peace. Tact was seldom a congressional attribute.

The militia was the chief beneficiary of this point of view, and most states, including New Jersey, preserved a semblance of efficiency in their local forces in the postwar years. This was true even after the inauguration of national government. While the new government had some strong advocates of a capable regular army, the view that a standing army was dangerous (and for that matter, the lack of money to pay for one) prevented the Washington administration from fielding more than a handful of regulars, and these saw most of their duty in the West against the Indians. National military policy, embodied in the Uniform Militia Act of 1792, still looked to the states to mobilize militia outfits for national service in periods of need. This act, however, like too many state militia laws, contained few provisions to assure adequate training and command, or even the use of standard equipment. The Militia Act tacitly continued the view that free men had an obligation to serve when called to the colors, but it remained to be seen whether relying on state militia for national defense would work. Most former Revolutionary officers, including Washington, were pessimistic.

In at least one test—the Whiskey Rebellion—the central government was able to use militia forces effectively. In 1794, farmers in western Pennsylvania refused to pay federal whiskey taxes (distilling being one of the region's chief sources of income). After attempts at a peaceful solution, President Washington finally became convinced that the rebellion was a threat to the authority of the young national government and resolved to put the westerners down with force. He called out the militias of Virginia, Maryland, and New Jersey in September, and within two months the expedition had restored order without bloodshed. State Governor Richard Howell led the New Jersey contingent and commanded a wing of the army. By all accounts, the New Jersey troops performed well in a campaign that fortunately did not lead to a civil war.

Aside from the Whiskey Rebellion there was little occasion to call militia units into national service. This was just as well, as even the march into Pennsylvania pointed to some of the limitations of the use of such troops. The government considered it inadvisable to call out Pennsylvania militia (would they have marched on fellow Pennsylvanians?); and the New Jersey contingent, labeled "militia," was not an existing state unit. Rather, it consisted of men recruited out of militia outfits and other volunteers. It had more in common with the troops raised for long-term duty in the colonial and Revolutionary eras than it did with any force of citizen-farmers concerned with local defense. Washington and the dominant Federalist Party harbored grave reservations about the militia. To the extent a reluctant Congress would allow, they raised a small corps of regulars for duty in the West. These troops, as well as territorial militia (which were little better than pickup outfits whose performance generally confirmed the worst fears about using militia for serious operations), fought a series of grueling and sometimes disastrous campaigns against the Indians in the Northwest Territory.

Former New Jersey residents who drifted to the frontiers, including an unknown number of Revolutionary War veterans, were caught up in this fighting, some of them seeing years of duty. Samuel Marsh, a private who had fought in the old First New Jersey at Monmouth, Yorktown, and other battles, was a case in point. He was present when the Miami and allied tribes smashed separate American armies under generals Josiah Harmar and Arthur St. Clair in Indiana, and when Anthony Wayne's critical victory at Fallen Timbers opened the way to peace in 1794. A poor man like many other veterans of the Revolution and the wars of the young republic, he settled into a meager civilian living only after years of army life. But in his day, he had helped to secure independence while in New Jersey and then to assure America's future in the West.

In the late 1790s, the so-called Quasi-War with France sparked a more ambitious attempt to raise federal regulars. Republican France, angered over the American refusal to come to its side against Britain, opened hostilities at sea. The fledgling American Navy generally did well in several fierce ship-to-ship duels. Though few Americans were convinced that the French were really likely to invade, the Adams administration prepared for war on land. In 1799, Aaron Ogden, a junior officer in the old New Jersey Brigade and a future governor, recruited a federal regiment in the state (the Eleventh United States Infantry). It never fought the French, but the regiment stayed on the roster, part of the American buildup before the War of 1812. Thus if official and popular rhetoric portrayed American arms in terms of militia—the "embattled farmers"—government practice increasingly emphasized the value of trained professional regiments.

The War of 1812

New Jersey, which saw so much of war during the Revolution, was not a battlefield during the War of 1812. Yet the struggle had a profound impact on the state. Since 1800, the Jeffersonian Republicans had dominated state politics. Joseph Bloomfield,

who had been a major in the Third New Jersey during the
Revolution and a general of state militia in the Whiskey Rebellion, was the state's popular and astute governor. Although
he disliked the British, he had reservations about President
James Madison's decision to declare war. Public opinion,
Bloomfield (and other Republicans) knew, was divided on the
matter, and in New Jersey the controversy was especially ran-
corous. Most of the support for the war lay in the South and
the West; the more commercial East, whose interests were open
to attack by the British Navy, was often less than enthusiastic.
The state Federalist Party flatly opposed a war, as did the
numerous Quakers in West Jersey, and even some good Jef-
fersonians pondered the wisdom of hostilities. In fact, Madison
had left some serious questions unanswered: How would America fight the world's greatest navy? What would conflict do to
regional mercantile and manufacturing interests? Where would
America find enough troops? Nevertheless, when the war came,
Bloomfield accepted a federal general's commission—leaving
the governor's seat vacant and open to a Federalist challenge.

The political reaction to the war matched the worst Republican predictions. The Federalists carefully cultivated antiwar sentiments, allied themselves with propeace Republicans
and pacifist Quakers, and swept both houses of the legislature
for the first time in a decade. They proceeded to elect Aaron
Ogden governor, and then enacted a peace agenda that stopped
little short of giving aid and comfort to the enemy. Branding
the war "inexpedient, ill-timed, and most dangerously im-
politic," the legislature tried to forbid New Jersey militia to
leave the state, even for the defense of New York City and
Philadelphia.[1] Taking their cue from the Federalists, some
militia ultimately went grumbling to New York, but only after
officers threatened to shoot recalcitrants.

Extreme Federalists, however, misjudged Governor Ogden.
Although he was against the war, the Revolutionary veteran
refused to condone disgracing American arms, and he took
seriously his job as commander in chief of New Jersey militia.
He saw to it that militia units garrisoned coastal areas, tried
to comply with national requests for militia reinforcements,
wrangled $5,000 out of the legislature for military purposes, and
stubbornly refused to go along with his party's wish to sabotage
the war effort. The battle between the governor and the

legislature soon cost the Federalists dearly. The infighting broke the antiwar coalition, and in 1813 the voters decisively returned the Republicans to office. The election placed the New Jersey Federalists on the road to political obscurity.

While the politicians fought their battles, the war went on, ultimately calling some six thousand New Jerseyans to duty in the national army and navy and in the militia. Most of these men served in the militia, and they saw little action. The enemy threat came from the sea, as the Royal Navy blockaded the coast from Sandy Hook to Cape May. There were several confrontations close offshore as local privateers or national vessels clashed with the enemy, and by 1815, several British and American ships had run aground and burned as a result of such actions. Fearful of British landings, the militia constructed fortifications at exposed points along the coast. Luckily, however, the local soldiery never had to defend their positions.

Yet if there was no major fighting at home, New Jersey also sent its men to the active fronts. In a war that generally brought few laurels to American arms, New Jersey citizens saw duty in victory and defeat, and many of them served with distinction. The state contributed, for example, most of the recruits for the Fifteenth United States Infantry, which the rest of the army unofficially called "the New Jersey regiment." Raised in the prewar build-up, the Fifteenth Infantry compiled a gallant record, especially in the 1813 invasion of Canada. Attached to General Bloomfield's First Brigade, the regiment was under the command of Colonel Zebulon M. Pike of Somerset County. Pike had led a Western exploration before the war, and Pike's Peak in Colorado bears his name. He led the Fifteenth and Sixteenth regiments in a successful assault on York (modern Toronto, Ontario), only to die in a magazine explosion after the city's surrender. A more fortunate New Jerseyan was General Winfield Scott, a young and capable officer. In 1814, his hard fighting at Chippewa and Lundy's Lane in Canada, across Lake Ontario from Buffalo, restored a measure of confidence to the American military.

There was also major fighting at sea, and New Jersey was associated with two of the most dramatic ship-to-ship duels of the war. On December 29, 1812, Commodore William Bainbridge of Princeton commanded the famed frigate* *Constitution* in an evenly matched fight against HMS *Java*. It was a brutal slugging contest, and the two ships traded broadside for broadside until better American gunnery sent the *Java* to the bottom. Bainbridge found himself celebrated as a hero, his exploit a contrast to American disappointments ashore. The Princeton officer went on to adistinguished career in the postwar Navy.

Burlington County gave the nation one of its best fighting sailors in Captain James Lawrence. A veteran of the naval campaign against the Barbary pirates during the Tripolitan War (1801–1805), Lawrence led the sloop *Hornet* to victory against the British brig *Peacock* early in 1812. In June, however, his luck ran out. In Boston harbor with a larger command, the frigate *Chesapeake,* he received a challenge from Captain Philip Broke of HMS *Shannon,* which was blockading the city. Broke wanted to fight "ship to ship, to try the fortunes of our respective flags," and Lawrence sailed to meet him. This was more gallant than intelligent, for the *Chesapeake*'s crew was only partially trained while the *Shannon*'s was one of the king's best. In a furious exchange, the British frigate shot the American to pieces and mortally wounded her captain. "Don't give up the ship," the dying Lawrence pleaded. "Fight her till she sinks."[2] The *Chesapeake* struck her colors anyway, but the New Jersey captain's "Don't give up the ship" passed into history as the battle cry of the United States Navy.

The battles of soldiers and sailors like Winfield Scott and William Bainbridge were sources of pride for the nation, but the fates of Zebulon Pike and James Lawrence were more indicative of the war effort. Only hard fighting, including naval victories on lakes Erie and Champlain, prevented disasters in the Northwest and in operations in New York State. American hopes of taking Canada vanished forever. Finally, in August 1814, a British army sent the government into flight and burned Washington, D.C. The Treaty of Ghent, which brought peace in 1815, was a diplomatic triumph of sorts for America if only because the British failed to exact any territorial concessions. More ironic was General Andrew Jackson's victory at New Orleans, fought after the signing of the peace treaty, which allowed the United States to end the conflict on a positive note. Even so, there was little hiding the fact that the War of 1812 had been a gigantic disappointment: American arms had narrowly avoided catastrophe.

The United States dismantled its military quickly after the

Captain James Lawrence. *Killed when he sailed his ill-prepared* Chesapeake *to a duel with HMS* Shannon *in 1813, Lawrence, of Burlington, became one of the relatively few publicly admired heroes of the War of 1812. Modern Lawrenceville is named for him.* COURTESY THE NEW JERSEY HISTORICAL SOCIETY.

end of hostilities. The country had done the same after the Revolution, and many Americans still regarded the maintenance of an army in peacetime as a threat to liberty. Besides, after 1815 the country was generally free of entanglements with Europe (which was one of the positive results of the war), and there arguably was no need for a major military establishment.

The militia went home, most of the Navy's ships were decommissioned, and the regular regiments, like New Jersey's Fifteenth Infantry, were consolidated into a peacetime force authorized at no more than 10,000 men. These troops were to spend most of their time in scattered coastal garrisons and on the nation's frontier, which was now pushing beyond the Mississippi River. Military affairs receded from public concern as America entered a period of unprecedented internal growth and westward expanion.

War Changes Its Face: The Rise of Industrialism and Professionalism

Even as Americans demobilized, however, new forces already were shaping the future course of warfare. By 1815, the industrial revolution was gathering momentum, with incalculable military consequences, and the vast new spaces opening to American settlement raised defense questions unanswerable by the nation's old militia tradition. Military planning in such a changing context would transform the armed forces over the next generation.

Until the Civil War, the regular American army remained small. A postwar depression compelled a further reduction in strength—down to 6,000 men—and the federal government, despite considerable thought on the matter, never devised a satisfactory approach to expanding its forces quickly in emergencies. Significantly, even if the idea of the citizen-soldier was still described in glowing terms publicly, most civilian officials and military men had given up on the militia. The local units had done poorly during the War of 1812. How were they to defend coastal cities against modern navies or guard scattered frontier farms against the Indians? Time-honored notions of democratic military obligations received short shrift, and the army focused on doing the best it could with its core of regulars. As practical reliance on the militia declined, many states neglected their local forces. New Jersey was typical in this regard. Training became infrequent and enrollment requirements went by the board. Eventually, some of the older militia outfits reorganized. Some became volunteer units; others set up as fire companies, assuming a useful role in the state's growing cities. Civilian and even militia contact with the regular army became minimal. There were small garrisons in the New York harbor posts, and army engineers and fatigue parties worked occasionally on the coastal defense positions on Sandy Hook (named Fort Hancock later in the century). Martial affairs may have counted for less during this period in New Jersey than at any other time in the state's history.

Yet the smaller more professional military was anything but static; rather, West Point graduates adapted advancing technology to their needs. The coastal defense positions on Sandy Hook were a case in point: The federal government approved these and other fortifications after British naval actions had demonstrated how exposed American ports were to seaborne attack. Work continued on them up to the Civil War. They required advanced military engineering and sophisticated gunnery, skills that trained professionals, not militia, possessed. By the 1830s and 1840s the military implications of such developments as the railroad and the telegraph were becoming clear as well, and technology was advancing rapidly in weapons production. In the early 1840s, following European practices, the army began phasing out flintlock muskets in favor of percussion cap weapons, and rifles became standard issue in the 1850s. The impact of these changes was not immediately apparent, but they would play havoc with massed infantry formations in the 1860s.

There were also advances at sea. In fact, improved naval technology had already had an impact during the War of 1812. Poor James Lawrence never knew it, but the *Shannon* had beaten him using advanced gunnery techniques not yet available to the American navy. After the war, however, the Americans did some innovating of their own. With Navy support, Captain Robert F. Stockton, another Princeton resident, collaborated with the Swedish inventor John Ericson (who later designed the Civil War ironclad* USS *Monitor*) in the building of the revolutionary USS *Princeton,* the world's first propeller-driven warship. She made paddle steamers, whose paddles were highly vulnerable to enemy fire, obsolete. Naval gunnery also evolved as solid-shot guns gave way to more powerful weapons firing exploding shells. Such progress, however, had its cost. In 1844, in a demonstration firing aboard the *Princeton,* a Stockton-designed gun exploded, killing the secretary of the navy, the secretary

of state, and a number of other civilians and sailors. It was a grim reminder that technology was making war ever more deadly.

An even grimmer prospect loomed: What would be the consequences if well-trained armies employed these new skills and technologically inspired weapons on a large scale? The answer became apparent during the Civil War—and had it become apparent earlier, one wonders if Americans would have flocked to the colors so readily in 1861. As it was, however, the next American war was against Mexico. Some of the new weapons saw duty, and the quality of military leadership proved superb; but if the conflict was bloody enough at times, the scale of the war was never such that the nation recoiled from the slaughter.

The Mexican War

The war with Mexico was a direct result of America's westward expansion. Well before the conflict, many Americans had resolved that the republic's "Manifest Destiny" was to span the continent from ocean to ocean. Voices of this persuasion freely argued that Mexican territory in Texas, the Southwest, and California must come under the Stars and Stripes (as would Oregon, which the United States occupied jointly with Great Britain); it would mean "extending the area of freedom." Mexico, however, did not see it this way. A proud young republic in the 1840s, Mexico had already lost Texas in a civil war and was not about to sit still as America threatened its pride and its provinces. The final straw came in 1845: the United States

OPPOSITE:
Militia Drill, Camp Washington, Near Trenton, 1840s. During the early 1840s the state militia was largely ineffectual. Volunteer militia units, which met to drill on a fairly regular basis, were better prepared. They were hardly ready to fight, but at least they were organized, knew basic maneuvers, and had some equipment. When New Jersey troops volunteered for duty in the Mexican War, many came out of the volunteer organizations. This print shows troops at drill in a camp outside Trenton. Drills often drew civilian spectators. COURTESY THE NEW JERSEY HISTORICAL SOCIETY.

annexed Texas (whose independence Mexico had never recognized) and, having settled the Oregon question peacefully with Britain, moved troops to the Rio Grande River, far into ground that Mexico had never considered part of Texas in the first place. Inevitably, shooting incidents occurred and President James K. Polk declared war in 1846.

The declaration of war brought a howl of protest from many Americans. There had been an organized peace movement in the country since 1815, and its ranks voiced articulate complaints; the war, they charged, was naked aggression. Antislavery Americans joined in the condemnation, seeing the war only as a southern ploy to add more slave territory to the Union. Opposition to the war was strongest in New England, where much of the protest centered in the Whig Party. But there were protests elsewhere, including New Jersey. The state generally supported the war effort, but the Whig majority in the legislature passed a resolution against the spread of slavery into any territory acquired from Mexico. Even army officers who would do their duty with genuine gallantry had major qualms. In his memoirs, no less than Ulysses S. Grant branded the war unjustified, a case of a stronger nation despoiling a weaker one.

Amid such controversy, Polk could hardly have called for troops based on any obligation of a citizen to serve. In fact, the administration made no pretense of calling for militia; the Mexican war was to be a war of regulars and volunteers. It was the first time that an American government had ignored the militia, although Washington did ask for state assistance in raising the volunteers. The secretary of war asked New Jersey to furnish a regiment, and Governor Charles C. Stratton issued a proclamation to do so in May 1846. Stratton, like Polk, turned to volunteers rather than militia. The latter, he noted candidly, were in a "defective and prostrate condition."[3] If New Jersey had needed its militia outfits "to suppress insurrection or repel invasion," the governor concluded, the situation would have been impossible. But the call for volunteers was a success. The response showed clearly that if many in New Jersey opposed the war, many more favored it. Companies offered their services from around the state, taking such picturesque names as the Lafayette Guards (Newark), the Jersey Guards (Burlington), the Washington Erina Guards (also Newark), the Flemington Grays, and, reviving the old name, the Jersey Blues (Trenton).

Most sailed from New York in September 1847, and Jerseymen fought under Generals Zachary Taylor, who attacked across the Rio Grande, and Winfield Scott. It was Scott, the New Jersey War of 1812 veteran, who battered his way from Vera Cruz to Mexico City, finally forcing the Mexicans to sue for peace in 1848.

While Taylor and Scott moved into Mexico proper, other troops were at work farther west. General Stephen Watts Kearny, a New Jersey officer, led a column to Santa Fe, New Mexico. After organizing a territorial government there, he proceeded to California, which he proclaimed as part of the United States. Further up the California coast, American naval forces took Monterey and San Francisco. Richard Stockton, now a commodore, assumed command of the naval contingent and appointed a territorial administration. Thus, with little actual fighting, the vast Southwest and California were incorporated into the Union.

Back in New Jersey, residents followed war news eagerly. The American victories generated considerable enthusiasm, and the legislature passed a resolution in praise of General Taylor and presented ceremonial swords to a number of New Jersey officers. When the state's volunteers came home in August 1848, they were greeted as heroes. The cheering, however, was brief. As opponents of the war had predicted, the territories won from Mexico soon figured prominently in the growing controversy over the spread of slavery. The road the army had followed to Mexico City also led, as events would prove, to Fort Sumter.

CHAPTER FOUR

The Civil War:
The Context of Change

The Civil War, some historians have insisted, was the first "modern war." That is, both sides fought it with mass, popularly based armies and supported their armed forces with significant industrial and administrative efforts behind the lines. Walter Millis, in his brilliant military history, *Arms and Men* (1956), has cautioned against taking this view too far. Civil War armies often did not (or could not) deploy the latest weapons or technological innovations—especially in the resource-starved South—and tactics frequently remained rooted in the earlier nineteenth century. So did romantic notions about the gallantry of warfare and the enthusiastic patriotism that characterized legions of early volunteers on both sides.

But the conflict at least marked a major transition toward modern war. Governments with mass democratic or popular support had launched the struggle, and only the fervent "popular nationalism" of the period—an indisputably modern phenomenon—could explain the enthusiastic volunteering of the first year of the war.[1] Even when war-weariness and disillusionment set in later, the administrative, political, and logistical apparatus—including conscription*—in Washington and Richmond were sufficient to keep manpower and supplies moving to the front until the Confederacy essentially ran out of both. New technologies, notably the telegraph and steam power (on rail and river) played their parts, allowing the rapid dispatch of mobilization and operations orders and equipment requisitions, the timely movement of large troop formations and material to critical points, and the quick transmission of intelligence. Cap-and-ball rifles permitted infantry to kill each other at half a mile and to wreak slaughter on close-order troop concentrations. By the end of the war, rifle fire and improved (if that is the word) artillery had compelled attacking forces to open ranks and defenders to dig in. The trenches of Lee's men at Petersburg in 1864–65 were not terribly different from those on the Western Front in World War I.

Finally, as in later wars, there were no decisive campaigns: wounded armies used modern transport to reinforce and resupply, and came back to fight again. Victory depended not only on beating enemy battalions, but on destroying an opponent's ability to maintain troops in the field. This meant war on transportation systems, farms, manufacturing, commerce, anything that could supply an army with food and the sinews of war. Ultimately, it was a brand of warfare that put the civilian economy and social structure of the South on the firing line— the consequences of which became dismayingly clear as General William T. Sherman marched through Georgia and General Philip Sheridan laid waste the Shenandoah Valley of Virginia. In the end, the Union never did destroy the main Confederate armies in open battle; they surrendered after a devastated South could no longer sustain them. Many of the distinctions between civilian and military targets had disappeared, even as the scale of combat had taken a quantum leap; whereas in earlier days rival armies had sparred, now entire peoples went to war.

All of this signified a gruesome transition in the status of armies. In the seventeenth and eighteenth centuries, and even to an extent in the early nineteenth century, military organizations normally were small. They were agents of kings or governments that saw armies as keys to domestic power as much as the means of waging war abroad. Such armies were not necessarily loyal to the nation as a whole, nor did the populace generally identify with them. (Indeed, these forces often included contingents of mercenaries.) As highly trained soldiers, they were difficult to replace and expensive to maintain; accordingly, governments seldom squandered their military resources. High casualties meant the recruiting and equipping of new battalions, which could easily bankrupt a treasury. European leaders conducted military operations with this concern in mind until the late eighteenth century; patriot administrators learned the same hard lesson trying to keep the Continental Army in the field. Besides, even if governments had been able to afford the expenses of major wars, they had few guarantees that their citizens would submit for long to the bloody sacrifices of battle. The general public simply had too little sense of national mission to support the lavish expenditure of their sons in conflicts in which they felt no personal stake. And in fact, governments usually discouraged popular political participation. Wars were the activities of rulers, not the ruled. But by 1860, Western armies had become the instruments of democratic or nationalistic systems; that is, they were extensions of the national will itself. And if, through a popularly based or nationalistic regime, a people embraced a cause as its own, it could treat manpower as just another resource, to be expended like shot or powder in pursuit of the national goal. Revolutionary France and Napoleon had done so, and much of Europe followed suit. In the Civil War, it was America's turn.

The scale and ferocity of the Civil War—the vast armies mobilized, the sheer numbers of men killed and wounded, the voracious demands for money, supplies, and equipment, and the inability of either side to knock out the other in a quick and decisive campaign—took Unionists and Confederates by surprise. Even those most willing to resort to arms had failed utterly to predict this kind of national immolation. The scope of the conflict dwarfed previous American experience. When he moved against Mexico City in 1847, Winfield Scott had commanded only some five thousand men; on the third day at Gettysburg in 1863, Lee hurled nearly three times that many at the Union line in Pickett's Charge alone. During the Mexican War, America had put some 104,000 men into uniform at one time or another; but between 1861 and 1865, about 2,982,000 served in blue or gray. Of these, some 360,000 Yankees and over 260,000 Southerners died. Unknowingly, Americans had entered a grim new era of warfare.

A State Divided

As the crisis of the Union loomed in 1860, New Jersey was bitterly divided. In many respects, New Jersey reacted more like such "Border States" as Maryland, Delaware, and Kentucky than its Northern neighbors. Sympathy for the South was strong. Part of southern New Jersey lay below the Mason-Dixon Line, and over the years cultural and commercial ties with the deeper South had become important to the state. Slavery had never completely died. While various acts had provided for its gradual elimination, in 1860 there were still eighteen slaves or "bound apprentices" in the state. There was open hostility toward free blacks and abolitionists. So intense were these feelings that one Newark newspaper editor, reacting to South Carolina's secession, proclaimed abolitionism "a worse calamity than disunion."[2]

States' rights doctrine, deeply ingrained in the thinking of many Jerseymen, also promoted hostility to the federal cause. Even during the war the legislature persisted in denouncing what it considered to be Washington's encroachments on state sovereignty, including the military use of New Jersey railroads. In addition, there were important New Jersey economic links with the South. The state's factories turned out clothing for Southern slaves, saddlery, wagons, agricultural supplies, and other manufactured goods, much of which went by sea from Newark to Savannah, Georgia. New Jersey business leaders and workers had little desire to lose these markets.

It was no surprise, then, when New Jersey emerged as the only northern state not to give its entire electoral vote to Abraham Lincoln in 1860. He barely carried the state, by four electoral votes to three. Indeed, in December of that year, Commodore Richard Stockton of Mexican War fame told a peace gathering in Trenton that New Jersey should ask the North to give in to Southern demands. And while there was no mass support for actual secession, some prominent political leaders at least hinted at it. In April 1861, former Governor Rodman C. Price argued that New Jersey "should go with the South, from every wise, prudential and patriotic reason."[3]

Yet there were firm Union supporters in the state. One newspaper editor denounced Price's remarks as treasonous, while others decried secession and urged the national government to end the rebellion through force of arms. If Lincoln did not sweep the state in 1860, he had articulate supporters; in February 1861, enthusiastic crowds gave him a rousing reception as he traveled across the state on the way to his inauguration. Pro-Confederates also received a setback with the April

12 Confederate attack on Fort Sumter in Charleston Harbor: most of New Jersey responded with cries of indignation and pledges of loyalty to the Union. For the time being, this patriotic reaction stilled all but the most vociferous critics of Lincoln and resulted in a flood of enlistments that took even Lincoln supporters by surprise. Grumbling continued—and later protests against the war flared to alarming levels—but New Jersey remained in Northern ranks.

Of those who stood for the Union, few did more than Governor Charles S. Olden. A conservative Whig, he won a narrow electoral victory in 1859 as the standard-bearer of the "Opposition Party," which finally became the state Republican Party near the end of the war. He opposed the extension of slavery but believed that each state should deal with the question for itself. He hoped fervently for a peaceful compromise to end the sectional crisis, but when Confederate guns opened on Fort Sumter he quickly took advantage of the state's patriotic enthusiasm and put New Jersey on a war footing. He called a special session of the legislature, and with bipartisan support he initiated measures to finance recruiting, purchase arms, and provide relief for the families of those in ranks. Thanks in large part to the governor's efforts, New Jersey sent considerably more men into the army in 1861 than the federal government had requested. Olden always considered New Jersey a border state, and he consequently looked askance at the Emancipation Proclamation when President Lincoln signed it in 1862. Nevertheless, he worked tirelessly to support President Lincoln's military effort and urged an aggressive conduct of the war. He saw to it that New Jersey regiments were reasonably well-equipped and that their officers were the best he could find and not political hacks. When Olden left office in January 1863, he was succeeded by Joel Parker, a Peace Democrat. The early nonpartisan support for the war had long since shattered. However, Olden continued to speak out on behalf of Union victory, and he could claim credit for being as responsible as anyone for making New Jersey a factor in the final triumph.

The unity that buoyed pro-Union spirits in 1861, as well as Governor Olden's war measures, could not endure federal military setbacks and revived antiwar political assaults. The New Jersey Republican Party was poorly organized and riven with internal factions; during the war it never controlled state government. Its ability to defend the war effort or the national administration, particularly during the many dark periods of military failure, was minimal. On the other hand, the state's conservative Democrats were firmly entrenched in the governor's mansion and in the legislature after the elections of 1862. While some Democrats loyally supported the war, many more, while attached to the Union, persistently criticized Lincoln's conduct of military affairs. Still other Democrats favored a quick peace and even recognition of the Confederacy, and their numbers included many overt "copperheads," who either espoused the Southern cause or otherwise openly opposed Union victory. Antiwar voices bided their time in the months after Fort Sumter, but when disaster struck Union arms at the Battle of Bull Run in July 1861, they renewed the chorus of discord.

The more extreme Peace Democrats seized on the Bull Run defeat—and the subsequent course of the war—to denounce the Lincoln administration and all of its works. The Newark *Daily Journal* trumpeted that "the North is destined to sure defeat." At various times, other editors and politicians gave open or thinly veiled encouragment to the rebels, denounced emancipation and abolition, praised slavery, and called for peace at virtually any price. In September 1862, the Emancipation Proclamation brought howls of Democratic protest (even some Republicans thought the measure extreme), and copperheads did their worst to stir up racial hatred and opposition to a war they labeled a "fanatical" cause. By any measure, such statements tested the outer limits of dissent during the Union's fight for life and, at least in Republican eyes, earned New Jersey the epithet of "the Copperhead State."

Antiwar sentiments peaked in 1863–64, fueled by the often dismal performance of the Union armies (including horrific casualty reports) and the issue of conscription. New Jersey had denounced heatedly any plans to conscript its citizens, arguing that the measure was a violation of states' rights, and as early as 1862 even some antiwar Democrats had urged greater efforts to recruit volunteers as a means to forestall a draft. But in March 1863, Lincoln announced his intention to begin drafting men during the summer, and attempts to enforce the law led to large-scale and bloody rioting in New York City in July. The violence abated and the draft began only after troops from the Army of the Potomac put down the rioters by force. Significant violence did not spread across the Hudson, although there were sizeable antidraft demonstrations in a number of northern New Jersey communities. The same year, the legislature passed resolutions urging an immediate peace, and the state senate revealed itself as openly hostile to the war effort.

Finally, in 1864, New Jersey supported a native son, General George B. McClellan, for president. McClellan, who had settled in West Orange after Lincoln relieved him of command of the Army of the Potomac, had received the Democratic nomination under peculiar circumstances: the party platform called for an end to the war, implying that the fighting should stop even at the cost of Union victory. While McClellan had no use for Abraham Lincoln, he considered his own party's stand on the war dishonorable and he had courage enough to renounce the Democratic platform. He lost the election, but New Jersey was one of three states to deny Lincoln its votes. (The former general was not through politically, however; in 1877 New Jersey voters elected him governor. He served one term until 1880.) It is worth noting, however, that New Jersey troops never had the chance to record their opinions of their former commander's presidential bid. New Jersey never came up with a workable plan to permit its soldiers to vote in the field—and did not approve one until ten years after the war. Most other states had no such difficulty, and their troops generally voted for "Ole Abe."

The state's venomous politics, however, did little to disrupt the machinery of war. The Lincoln administration was a legitimately elected government, and as long as it retained command of the national political and military apparatus, its agents continued to raise men, money, and supplies despite the feelings of any individual state. Even a highly disaffected state government such as New Jersey's limited its protests just to heated resolutions and rhetoric. Such protests could be dangerous, but they did not include steps to disrupt recruiting or military operations. Any such measures would have drawn a strong federal legal or military response. Military policy had become a national matter; states had become part of the vastly larger system (notably in their recruiting operations), but the day was past when a state, short of rebellion, could seriously contest national prerogatives in this area.

Most of Lincoln's critics in New Jersey were not willing to

carry their protests beyond words and votes. Governor Joel Parker was a case in point. A former militia general and a conservative Democrat, Parker won election in 1862 while proclaiming himself opposed to both secession and emancipation. In office he stood for states' rights, castigated the conduct of the war, and supported McClellan's candidacy in 1864. But he never acted to obstruct the military. Indeed, in objecting to the draft in 1863, he carefully avoided actions that would have impeded enlistments. Instead, he convinced Washington to let him reorganize local efforts to recruit volunteers, and New Jersey ultimately filled its quotas for 1863 without resorting to conscription; drafting began instead in 1864. He was also conscientious in the appointment of officers for state regiments and, in times of crisis, proved willing to communicate directly with the president. Republicans fumed over his criticism of Lincoln, while Copperheads denounced his failure to actively oppose the conduct of the war. But he won the applause of most regular Democrats, and his career illustrated how New Jersey dissent became an uneasy but constant companion of the war effort.

The Fighting Front

The public airing of political differences perhaps overshadowed a deeper popular attachment to the Union. New Jersey citizens proved willing enough to fight, and they warmly supported early Union mobilization efforts (the largest to that point in national history). The regular Army numbered only some 16,000 men in late 1860, and the president had to call on the states to provide volunteers to augment national forces. Enlistments began in early 1861, after Lincoln asked for 75,000 men to serve for three months, and recruiting accelerated progressively as it became clear that the Confederacy would not die a quick death. Ten thousand volunteers from the Garden State—three times the New Jersey quota—answered Lincoln's initial call. Patriotism, the lure of bounties, and, after 1864, a draft kept recruits moving to the fronts. By the end of the war more than 88,000 Jerseymen had served ashore or afloat for the Union, over 10,000 more than the national government had requested. Of these, some 6,300 never came back.

While most of the New Jersey troops, particularly those

enlisted after 1861, served in new volunteer regiments, the state militia played an important role as well. However, it was no longer a militia fielded on the old colonial or Revolutionary principle of a citizen's obligation to serve. That militia structure had proved unworkable during the Mexican War, and in the 1850s Governor Rodman Price—who later spoke so vehemently on behalf of the South—had reorganized the state units on a volunteer basis. Part-time volunteers drilled much as National Guard troops do today. While these troops were hardly veterans, the New Jersey Adjutant General* had instilled some discipline: units drilled with regularity, knew basic maneuvers, and could handle their weapons. Price's reforms also included the encouragement of immigrant enlistments, primarily among the Irish and Germans. In what historian Joel Schwartz has termed "a subtle revolution in the ranks," he commissioned many ethnic officers, which broadened the popular base of military participation and had the implicit effect of drawing immigrant groups more fully into national life—a fact of no mean importance in 1861.[4] When Unionist Governor Olden called New Jersey to the colors after Fort Sumter, the existence of these volunteer militia made the task immeasurably easier, and there was more than a little irony in the fact that he made such effective use of units organized in large part by the pro-Southern Price.

Mustered into the national army, the new regiments fought under federally appointed generals, but throughout the war most volunteer commanders up to the grade of colonel won their rank from their home states. In this respect, the governors did retain a certain amount of practical military influence. The volunteer regiments also maintained their state designations: the First New Jersey Volunteers, the Twenty-sixth New Jersey Infantry, the First New Jersey Brigade, the Second New Jersey Calvary, and so forth. War was nationalizing and modernizing, but some local touches remained.

New Jersey soldiers and sailors saw action throughout the war, compiling a record that became a source of pride even to many who doubted the wisdom of the conflict. Sailors served on the scattered shore stations, in fleets blockading Southern ports, and on the river boats that supported Union operations along the western and midwestern rivers. Most of the troops fought in the East, attached to the Army of the Potomac and

Militia Roster, Civil War. *Volunteer units frequently printed lavishly illustrated rosters, seeking to honor the early troops who answered the call to march against the Confederate States. The roster of the 15th New Jersey Volunteers, an infantry regiment, was typical. The 15th, raised in 1862, initially had 940 officers and enlisted men. It saw its first action in the Union defeat at Fredericksburg, Virginia, where it suffered only light casualties. However, it fought in virtually all of the battles of the Army of the Potomac, and by late 1864 it could muster fewer than 200 men of all ranks.* COURTESY THE NEW JERSEY HISTORICAL SOCIETY.

allied forces. The New Jerseyans shared the fortunes of this famed but often hard-luck command, and they marched with it to the first disaster at Bull Run and on to the final and victorious Appomattox Campaign. The combat history of Garden State servicemen, however, remains to be written— there is no comprehensive account of their operations. Yet there are hundreds of printed and manuscript records of the fighting on land and afloat. Ranging from regimental histories to the diaries and letters of individual officers and men, each provides part of a story too vast to attempt here. A few examples, however, indicate the scope of the conflict and the profound impact it had on those in ranks and on those who waited for them back home.

USS Cumberland, Hampton Roads, Virginia, March 8, 1862

On the afternoon of March 8, the Confederate ironclad *Virginia* steamed into Hampton Roads to confront the blockading Northern fleet. The Union ships had expected the rebel to sortie* and had hoped to have an ironclad of their own—USS *Monitor*—to meet her. But the *Monitor* would not be on hand until the next day (when it fought its epic duel with the *Virginia*), and the wooden men-of-war* had to look to themselves. The squadron flagship was the steam frigate the *Cumberland*, forty guns, and the *Virginia* headed for her. The federal vessel opened fire as the ironclad closed, only to have its shot bounce off the Confederate's armor. The *Virginia*'s first return fire killed nine men, and the carnage increased with every additional salvo.* After pounding the *Cumberland* with gunfire for fifteen minutes, the Southerner rammed the wounded frigate, which went under even as her captain refused a surrender demand: "Never!" he replied. "We will sink with our colors flying."[5]

As the brief battle drew to a close, Lt. Commander John L. Lenhart, chaplain of the stricken *Cumberland*, did his best to help the wounded and dying (and there were all too many: of the ship's complement of 376, over 120 were fatalities). A Methodist minister in New Jersey for over a decade, Lenhart had served congregations in Flemington, Long Branch, Mount Holly, Bridgeton, Camden, Newark, and Paterson before accepting a chaplain's commission in 1847. He generally had enjoyed his fifteen years of Navy life, and he did not flinch at the prospect of battle at Hampton Roads. Shortly before the fight he wrote about the realization that battle was imminent. "We felt ready for them, and I am not sure but a goodly number of us felt desirous to have them come on."6 One wonders if he recalled these sentiments as the blasted *Cumberland* began to sink. What is certain, however, is that Chaplain Lenhart thought little of his own safety. Survivors reported his assisting the wounded as comrades brought them below deck, and as the rising water threatened to engulf them all, his refusal to leave the injured men to their fate. Instead, unhurt himself, he stayed to the end and went down with the ship. He was the first chaplain in Navy history to die in battle.

First New Jersey Volunteers, Gaines's Mill, Virginia, June 27, 1862

Between April and June 1862, General George B. McClellan cautiously worked the Army of the Potomac up the Yorktown Peninsula toward the rebel capital of Richmond. It was a steady if unspectacular advance, and Private Alfred Lyman Lincoln was more bored than frightened. A native of Connecticut, where he still had family, Lincoln had enlisted after Fort Sumter with the First New Jersey Volunteers at Hoboken. He had rallied to the colors, as a New Jersey comrade recalled, when "the boom of the traitorous gun . . . sent defiance to the Nation."7 Lincoln's regiment was attached to a brigade under New Jersey General Philip Kearny, a man who knew how to fight; but Alfred's letters home during early 1862 complained less of Confederate bullets than of bad weather and Virginia mud. On June 25 a Southern counterattack (the beginning of the famous Seven Days' Battles) stopped McClellan and forced him to begin a slow retreat. As McClellan pulled back, the Confederates struck again on the 27th at Gaines's Mill, where the First New Jersey took a beating and Private Lincoln more than made up for any excitement he had missed earlier. He stopped a bullet, and his company left him for dead on the battlefield.

Since it was not War Department practice to telegraph the families of men lost in action, it generally fell to a soldier's comrades to bear the sad news to loved ones back home. Private Edward Hollinger wrote to Lincoln's brother, Edwin, informing him of Alfred's probable death. Edwin's response, which conveyed the anguish of an almost inconsolable family, was sadly typical of many such letters:

> Indeed no language can express my feeling on learning that my brother, my best and dearest friend, now is sleeping in the cold embrace of death in an unknown grave. May he rest in peace. Kind sir, this is to me a heavy blow, the saddest of my life. . . . But now those bonds of brotherly affection are severed by cruel death, never again to be united in the world of tears. O this is a heavy trial to bear, but mourning can not recall him therefore I must endeavor to feel resigned to my loss and it is some consolation to think that he fell while bravely fighting to maintain the honor of this country's flag. But his poor afflicted mother will mourn his death even more than myself. . . . Write all the particulars concerning my brother you can gather and I will thank you. . . . Though according to your statement he was in all probability killed instantly but still as your captain only saw his fall it is possible that he is only severely wounded and fell into the hands of the enemy.[8]

Edwin's hope proved true: Alfred, wounded in the shoulder, had fallen prisoner. After he was exchanged, Private Lincoln recovered and served until the end of his enlistment—despite the pleas of his sister to seek a medical discharge. Yet he was not the same enthusiastic volunteer who had signed on in Hoboken. His letters took a sober turn, and he once complained to Edwin about "the deceitfullness of mankind in general." He would still fight, but he was weary of the camps, the shirkers, and the fact that "life has so few charms."[9] The romance of the war was gone.

Eleventh New Jersey Infantry, Gettysburg, July 2, 1863

After a day of inconclusive fighting, the Army of Northern Virginia and the Army of the Potomac faced one another along two lines of high ground outside the town of Gettysburg. The Southerners occupied Seminary Ridge while Union troops, under George Gordon Meade, held Cemetery Ridge. Near midafternoon a corps under Union General Daniel Sickles moved forward half a mile, searching for more defensible ground. The new position was an invitation to trouble—Sickles's flanks were exposed and he was too far from supporting Union formations—and at about 4:00 P.M. plenty of trouble arrived.

The Confederate First Corps, under General James Longstreet, stormed into Sickles's units and brought on one of the most desperate fights in American history. Longstreet's assault turned the Union line into a shambles, battered other units sent to help, and threatened a breakthrough that could well have made Gettysburg Lee's greatest triumph.

Fighting bitterly, the outnumbered men in blue fell back as comrades dropped around them. Longstreet's battalions surged through gaps in the Union line, hitting federal outfits with frontal and flank attacks* and shooting some of them to pieces. The Eleventh New Jersey got caught in the worst of it. Trying to change front to deal with a flank attack, the Eleventh's Colonel Robert McAllister, a Warren County railroad construction engineer before the war, went down just as he gave orders to fire. Another bullet dropped Major Philip J. Kearny almost as soon as he took command. The senior captain lived only seconds after he learned that he was now in charge. Captain Dorastus Logan fared no better. He was wounded as he took over the dissolving regiment, and as four enlisted men were trying to carry him off the field a blast of rifle fire finished them all. Two more captains were killed or wounded trying to steady what was left of the shattered command, which finally passed to a young lieutenant. Of the regiment's 275 men who went into action that afternoon, only 121 were in ranks by sundown.

By the end of the day, Longstreet's men had carried most of the field. They had beaten Sickles thoroughly, chewed up other units that had tried to support him, threatened the Army of the Potomac with calamity, and decimated regiments like the Eleventh New Jersey. But those regiments had gone down fighting, and they had not let Longstreet land a knockout punch. When the July 2 battle ended, what was left of the New Jersey regiment was still on the firing line and positions on Cemetery Ridge remained intact. Lee concluded that if he wanted to win, he would have to attack again. The next day he did—and in Pickett's Charge he lost the Confederate cause.

Appomattox Court House, Virginia, April 9, 1865

By late 1864, the war had entered its cruelest period. Places like the Wilderness, Cold Harbor, and Petersburg brought a

grim, modern visage to the face of combat. Set-piece battles—
that is, carefully planned engagements between major units in
the open field—became rare, replaced by almost continuous
contact with the enemy. Sniper fire and raids forced both sides
to dig in, and a deep bitterness permeated the armies. The
wounded died in brush fires or bled to death between the lines,
where their unburied bodies rotted. The war had become a
grinding affair, consuming men by scores or hundreds each day.
Had it known what to look for, the world could have seen an
early version of the Western Front in 1917. Still, neither side
would quit.

But the war ended. The relentless application of Union might
finally told, and without a cataclysmic last battle, a retreating
Army of Northern Virginia was brought to bay at Appomattox
Court House. At last, Robert E. Lee knew that he could do
no more and, no fanatic, he surrendered. Robert McAllister,
the New Jersey officer who survived his Gettysburg wounds and
was now a general, reported the final act of the national drama
in words that cannot be improved:

> For four long years our armies had been battling for these
> glorious results, [in] the accomplishment of which thousands had
> been cut down and thousands more wounded and maimed for
> life. All knew that by the surrender of Lee and his army the
> great contest was over. The war was ended, and we could return
> to our homes with the proud satisfaction that it has been our
> privilege to live and take part in the struggle that has decided
> for all time to come that Republics are not a failure.[10]

The Home Front

Historians debate the impact of the Civil War on the national
economy, but there is a general consensus that the conflict
provided a major stimulus to industrialization. There is similar
agreement that industry expanded in New Jersey during the war
years, and certainly that state business and agriculture formed
an important part of the economic base that sustained the
military effort. Federal orders for military materiel poured into
the state, and New Jersey businesses became major suppliers
of clothing, flags, munitions, and heavy and finished goods.

Important components of the first Union ironclad, USS *Monitor* —including the novel turret rings which allowed her guns to swing a full circle—came out of a New Jersey factory. Orders for uniforms were so heavy that manufacturers (following a national trend) began producing in standard sizes for the first time on a mass basis, thus launching what became a regular feature of the clothing industry. By the end of the war, more state residents were working in industrial jobs of all kinds than ever before.

Agriculture shared in the war-related prosperity. New Jersey farms had produced record wheat crops in the 1850s, and the requirements of the military, as well as the growing regional industrial work force, for flour and related products kept demand for this crop strong. Potatoes, long a New Jersey product, came into their own as a major cash crop for similar reasons. Corn was also important, both as a cattle feed (and the state sold plenty of beef to the government) and for forage, vital for the vast numbers of cavalry and transport animals that kept the armies moving. Agricultural growth was such that the state legislature funded a curriculum in advanced agricultural techniques at the school that became Trenton State College. Under the federal Morrill Act of 1862, New Jersey designated Rutgers as a land-grant college, thus beginning one of the most successful efforts in agricultural education and research in the nation's history.

On a very immediate level, economic prosperity paid handsome dividends to the Union cause: it provided the sinews of war and, significantly, it took the edge off of antiwar dissent. As it became clear that military demand for New Jersey products would more than make up for lost Southern business, early business and labor fears about the war's impact on the state economy abated, and with them much of the opposition to the war. Yet there were other implications that became clear only in retrospect. For the first time in a modern sense, the state economy became inextricably bound to a national military effort. The war required the products of New Jersey farms and factories, while in turn those same farms and factories looked to war-driven demands to sustain their growth. The relationship was indicative of how complex military affairs had become, and how essential a strong civilian economy was in waging war over vast distances with huge armies and fleets that consumed mountains of supplies and relied on advanced equipment. The Union had such an economic base, and could protect it, and it won; the Confederacy had a smaller industrial foundation and could not protect it, and it lost. In the history of warfare, there had been few clearer lessons on the importance of the home front.

As the conflict took its deadly course, civilians eagerly followed the progress of battles and campaigns in the press. By the 1860s, newspapers were a truly mass medium; the state had eight daily or weekly papers, and almost all New Jersey residents had access to at least one of them. They had plenty to read, for the Civil War was reported like no other event in the young nation's history. While few of the journals could afford to attach special correspondents to the armies, they readily printed Associated Press wire stories, letters from the front, accounts from soldiers on leave or discharged, and government bulletins. As a rule, fact or truth was only a point of departure in reporting a story. As historian Alan Siegal has explained, the press was widely partisan—newspapers ranged from ardently pro-Lincoln to copperhead—and the editor's political point of view often determined the slant of a story. To the extent that editors sought to influence public opinion on the war the activities of the press served as yet another example of the importance of the home front.

The war made other demands on civilian New Jersey as well. Given the fact that so many families had men in the armed forces, many civilians donated their time and money to troop relief efforts. Care of the wounded—in the field and at home—and relief for disabled veterans and for their families was largely a concern of private charity, and many New Jerseyans rose to the occasion. Clara Barton, a former New Jersey schoolteacher, organized a supply effort to meet the needs of wounded soldiers, and later served as the superintendent of nurses with the Army of the James in Virginia and North Carolina. Women volunteers served with the United States Sanitary Commission, which cared for the wounded in military hospitals, contacted the families of sick and injured troops, and vastly improved camp and hospital sanitary conditions.

Near the end of the conflict, as federal arms ground down the Confederacy, and as thousands of state residents in and out of uniform played their parts for the Union, the political pendulum swung away from the Democrats. In 1865, Republican

Sanitary Commission Fair. *Organized to provide medical relief and social support for the Union troops, the Sanitary Commission operated on the home front in the Northern states. Composed of men and women volunteers, the commission raised money through fairs and other social functions to buy medical supplies, reading materials, and other amenities for those in uniform. Aside from war-related business activity, working with the Sanitary Commission offered one of the most direct ways a civilian could participate in the war effort. This picture shows a fund-raising fair in New Jersey.* COURTESY THE NEW JERSEY HISTORICAL SOCIETY.

Marcus L. Ward won a resounding gubernatorial victory. Ward had been active in war-related philanthropy and grateful veterans voted for him in droves. Under his leadership, New Jersey belatedly ratified the Thirteenth and Fourteenth amendments to the Constitution, which abolished slavery and took the first steps toward making justice color-blind in America. Ward's effort, as other Republicans joked, marked New Jersey's "return to the Union." Ward's term clearly illustrated the high point of popular support for the Union cause in the Garden State; the next election sent the Democrats back to the State House.

CHAPTER FIVE

The Military Hiatus: 1865 to the 1890s

The Civil War revealed much of the dawning era of total war. The impact of industry and science were tragically manifest: rifled small arms, improved artillery and explosives, armored ships, and better transport and communications had all written their stories in blood. Democratic participation in politics, use of mass media, and sophisticated party organization made it possible to mobilize the masses—and to continue that mobilization even as thousands went to slaughter. The deliberate assault on the civilian economy and social structure of the Confederacy also foreshadowed a full recognition that modern war was not just a contest between armies; it would pit entire peoples against one another. The prospect of warfare had become more frightening than ever.

Without pondering the implications of the question, most Americans seemed to realize the war had turned a terrible corner in history; certainly the end of the Civil War found them thoroughly sick of the bloodletting. It would be some time before anyone in public life would seriously suggest that the United States should resort to the sword to settle major disputes, and there was general agreement when General William Tecumseh Sherman pronounced that war was hell. The United States rapidly demobilized what had been the greatest war machine on earth, cutting the army to some twenty-five thousand men for frontier duty and the occupation of the South. The Navy sold off, decommissioned, or scrapped most of the fleet. Few in government gave much thought to any formal American military policy or considered that the country might again face a conflict of the magnitude of the War of the Rebellion. Indeed, for years the country showed little serious inclination to use the military as an instrument in international affairs, and for most Americans, things military receded from public view and concern.

On a more subtle level, however, military affairs remained an important part of national life. If the American military was small, it remained interested in what the rest of the world was doing; military missions to Europe monitored developments there, and individual officers and civilians took pains to assess how America might respond in the face of a martial crisis. Slowly but steadily, the nation's military modernized. In the 1870s, breech-loading rifles* and artillery* replaced muzzle-loaders,* and during the 1880s the army adopted new weaponry and advanced designs for coastal fortifications. At Fort Hancock on Sandy Hook, for example, masonry works, which modern naval guns would have blasted to rubble, gave way to concrete gun positions dug beneath ground level. The Navy, which had gone back to using sail after the Civil War, also took some progressive steps. USS *Trenton* became the first ship wired for electrical lighting, and by the 1880s Congress realized that the old wooden Navy was hopelessly obsolete. Reform was necessary if the country was to have anything in service that could float. Consequently, the Naval Appropriations Act of 1883 provided a modest building program for steel ships, better ordnance,* and steam power plants, and set a course for continued technical improvement during the rest of the century. Compared to the armed forces of Europe, American forces were quite small—there was no evident need for a larger military—but there was a growing awareness of the necessity of at least keeping up with technical advances.

There was also activity at the state level. By law, the old Militia Act of 1792 still governed state military organizations.

Yet the act had been a dead letter for decades, a lesson the
Civil War had driven home with finality. To the extent that they
bothered at all with their local forces, governors and legislators
continued to rely on volunteer units, a practice which took on
some troubling overtones as the 1870s advanced. It was an era
that saw considerable labor and civil unrest, and a number of
states used their regiments against strikes or other demonstrations. Indeed, some volunteer units had come together, often
with rank and file drawn from middle and wealthier
socioeconomic groups, with precisely such concerns in view.
While New Jersey avoided the violence of neighboring Pennsylvania, for example, which used troops against strikers in the
steel mills and coal mines, there was still trouble in the air.
In 1877, Governor Theodore F. Randolph used state forces to
put down rioting between rival railroad construction gangs in
Bergen County and threatened to use them to keep the peace
between feuding Catholic and Protestant Irish groups in Jersey
City. Under the command of an officer who was also superintendent of a Pennsylvania Railroad subsidiary, militia volunteers
moved into Phillipsburg during a strike there by Pennsylvania
Railroad workers. For a time, it seemed that domestic tumult,
rather than external threat, would provide the militia's *raison
d'etre*.

Many citizens, however, including many volunteer officers,
considered such a prospect appalling. In 1879, in a move reflect-
ing these concerns, as well as what many considered the
legitimate need of state governments to maintain domestic
tranquility (although, in fact, this often meant strikebreaking),
delegates from New Jersey and eighteen other states met in
New York to organize the National Guard Association. Out of
the gathering came the foundation of the modern National
Guard: state volunteer troops, available for local duty but with
the primary purpose of serving the regular military as reserves.
It took time for this mission to assume its full dimensions. Most
outfits were not trained for combat, nor were they equipped
for it, but the new interest in the guard ultimately deflected
calls for a force intended primarily to protect the wealthy.
Instead, it set a course toward a more positive role for the state
military in national and local affairs.

New Jersey's National Guard reflected this wider trend toward the creation of a genuine military reserve. During the late

1870s, Governor George B. McClellan—the man Lincoln had fired as commander of the Army of the Potomac—worked hard to expand the Guard and to improve its organization and discipline. He saw to it that drill became more regular, put another battalion on the books, and equipped two companies with Gatling guns.* Hardly a combat-ready organization, and lacking any real coordination with the regular army it was supposed to support, the guard at least maintained a schedule of training activities and was more than a shadow organization over the rest of the century. By the 1890s, the state also had a small but active naval militia. The key element in all of this was volunteerism: The old militia concept of universal obligation had, for the time being, lost any practical force in local military planning. Finally, a federal law formalized the role of the National Guard as a training and manpower volunteer pool for the national army. It left the guard under state control, but provided for uniformity in training and equipment and specified the conditions under which the nation could call the state troops to the colors. In theory, the National Guard would serve as the wellspring of legions of prepared citizen-soldiers in a national emergency.

Events of even greater long-term importance for the military, however, were taking place in the civilian economy. New Jersey economic development over the last quarter of the nineteenth century was of a piece with national industrial growth. New Jersey–based operations of such innovative firms as Standard Oil, Campbell Soup, Singer Sewing Machine, Roebling's Sons, United States Steel, and Thomas A. Edison's various companies expanded. Their work marked advances in textile manufacture, steel and iron work, food processing, tool design, petroleum refining, and basic and applied research—in short, all of the areas that America would need to support an expanded and technologically advanced military machine in the future. In fact, even the modest naval build-up of the 1880s and 1890s drew on New Jersey's steel-making capabilities. Not surprisingly, many New Jersey steel manufacturers became advocates of a "Big Navy" (to use the term of the period) when calls for massive additions to the fleet came near the end of the century.

This industrial growth did not deliberately take military possibilities into consideration. It came about as a result of Western capitalism developing around civilian markets and private investment. The economy had little need for the stimulation of military contracts or planning, and the potential of the military market became obvious only later. Even after the turn of the century, army and navy spending accounted for a small fraction of national or state industrial output. Yet the industrial and technical ability to support war on a scale bigger than anything imagined during the 1860s was in place, and so were the managerial skills. The corporate and industrial expansion had produced, as an inevitable by-product, much of the leadership the country would need for warfare in the industrial era.

The war America fought near the turn of the century was hardly a test of the nation's capabilities. The Spanish-American War was over quickly—fought between April and August of 1898—and in a seeming blaze of glory. The new American navy made short work of Spanish fleets in the Philippines and Cuba; and the army, despite some incredible logistical snafus,* functioned well enough to beat the Spaniards quickly in Cuba. Casualties were light—indeed, the United States lost more men to disease than to combat—and Secretary of State John Hay captured much of the popular mood when he referred to the conflict as the "splendid little war."

The war with Spain offered the first chance to call the National Guard into federal service in an international dispute. In mid-April, the national government asked New Jersey for three regiments, and Governor Foster M. Voorhees responded quickly. The naval militia came out quickly and some of its men saw action off Cuba. By early May, the state also had mobilized some three thousand members of the National Guard. They were organized at Sea Girt and then sent by the army to military stations in the United States, mostly in Florida. The war ended, however, before they could be deployed to Cuba or Puerto Rico. Historians have generally been critical of the country's attempt to call up the guard and to recruit volunteers, and it is true that too many local outfits lacked proper equipment, training, and organization. Most states could not match New Jersey's relatively efficient mobilization. Yet, had the war lasted longer, more men were available for action and no doubt would have seen it. As it was, enough men reached Cuba to get the job done.

Organizational difficulties, however, did prompt military re-

forms shortly after the war. In 1903, the same law that gave
federal sanction to the National Guard also created an American general staff, allowing the military to adopt many of the
management and planning skills of the civilian economy. The
new system was designed to improve the country's ability to
marshal human and material resources in wartime. The law
reflected military planning steps already adopted in most of
Europe—all of which would make possible the carnage of World
War I.

The brief encounter with Spain made the United States an
imperial power in the Caribbean and the Pacific. This development was an unpleasant surprise to many Americans, and an
articulate minority opposed the acquisition of colonies on moral
and political grounds. Such feelings intensified when Philippine

*Volunteer First Aid Crew, Spanish-American War. During the war against
Spain in 1898, New Jersey residents volunteered for noncombatant service
as well as for duty in the line of fire. This picture shows a first-aid crew
at Sea Girt, which served as an organizing base for the military during
the brief conflict.* COURTESY THE NEW JERSEY HISTORICAL SOCIETY.

G. THORN, PHOTO-ARTIST.

nationalists, who originally had hailed the American role in freeing them from Spain, launched a protracted war for independence. New Jersey reflected this national debate. A few voices said flatly that it was wrong to force American dominance on a people who wanted to be free. Others based their anti-imperialism on cconomics. In Newark, for example, cigar makers opposed the annexation of the Philippines, fearing competition from Filipino labor. Yet other state industries saw American expansion as an opportunity to increase markets in the Far East, and they forcefully supported the nation's imperial venture. In general, popular opinion, still euphoric over victory and enjoying the nation's new prestige, also supported annexation. Vice-President Garret A. Hobart, a shrewd Republican from Passaic County, was an articulate spokesman for the expansionist point of view, and he was influential in President William McKinley's ultimate decision to keep the Philippines.

This was pretty heady stuff for most Americans. Indeed, popular enthusiasm for war with Spain, and the willingness to move aggressively onto the colonial stage, was in marked contrast to the national mood after Appomattox. Gradually, time had softened the images of the Civil War: a new generation knew it only through the press, the stories of veterans, the activities of the Grand Army of the Republic (the veterans' organization of the period), and the proliferation of war memorials in town squares. The slow rebirth of interest in national military affairs in the 1880s, and the jingoism or belligerent nationalism of the latter 1890s, had also helped wipe

OPPOSITE:
Grand Army of the Republic Meeting. *The Grand Army of the Republic— or GAR—was a national organization of Union Army veterans. Organized with state and local chapters, the GAR lobbied state and federal governments for veterans' benefits and strove to influence the schools to teach a "patriotic" version of Civil War history (which meant a version conceding no virtue to the South or to those who opposed the war in the North). The GAR, with millions of members at its height, was a familiar part of community life from the 1880s through the 1930s; its meetings and public activities served as a visible reminder of the Civil War years. This picture shows veterans of the 2nd New Jersey Cavalry at a GAR meeting in Plainfield about 1890. PHOTO BY G. THORN, COURTESY M. LENDER.*

away the grim memories of the 1860s. There was virtually
nothing in what happened in Cuba or the Philippines to remind
the nation of the agony of Gettysburg or the cold and bitter
trenches of Petersburg. Americans would have to relearn these
lessons the hard way, which suggests that the most squalid
aspect of the Spanish-American War was that it restored a
measure of romance and adventure to warfare.

Black American Soldiers Decorated in Cuba. *The army was segregated
until after World War II, although black troops saw combat in all
American conflicts. Black outfits, which included volunteers from New
Jersey, took part in some of the toughest actions in Cuba in 1898. Here
officers of the Cuban forces in revolt against Spanish rule decorate some
of the black Americans. COURTESY THE NEW JERSEY HISTORICAL SOCIETY.*

CHAPTER SIX

War and Modern America

The carnage of the First World War caught most Americans by surprise. By late 1914, a line of trenches stretched across Western Europe, and over the next two years casualties soared into the millions. Industrialized armies, mass conscription, and careful management of mobilization and logistics plans, which the warring goverments had counted on to rout their enemies in weeks, had bogged down into the biggest slaughter in recorded history. In the United States, President (and former New Jersey Governor) Woodrow Wilson initially tried to keep the nation neutral. Despite a vocal minority that called for intervention on behalf of Britain and France, Wilson had the public with him. In 1916, he successfully ran for a second term behind the slogan "He Kept Us Out of War."

Even in neutrality the nation gradually found the war moving closer. The propaganda of the European powers competed for American public opinion, with the Allies (Great Britain, France, Italy, Russia) getting a better hearing. Incidents like the sinking of the British ocean liner *Lusitania,* with the loss of many American lives, certainly fed hostility to Germany. But in states like New Jersey, with large Italian, German, and Irish populations (the Irish, with their own problems with Britain, were often pro-German), the war bred ethnic tensions. Unpleasant enough themselves, these ethnic animosities sometimes got tangled up in other disputes. In 1915, for example, strikers at the Forstmann & Huffman Mills in Passaic questioned the loyalty of the company's German-American owners. The issue was a sham (although at least it was novel; the norm was for employers to question the loyalty of strikers), but the workers raised

75

another issue of greater interest: war profits. Forstmann & Huffman was in fact selling textiles to European governments, and in this practice the firm was typical. A thriving trade in war goods of all kinds buoyed the American economy, and New Jersey companies took full advantage. Most of the sales were to the Allies, with munitions taking the lead in the Garden State. DuPont, Hercules Powder, and other firms made fortunes; by 1918, after American entry into the war, New Jersey was the nation's largest munitions manufacturing center.

Several dramatic incidents brought this fact home with a vengeance. On July 30, 1916, railroad cars full of ammunition parked in the Black Tom section of Jersey City blew sky-high. The detonation, which may have been the work of German saboteurs, was so violent that towns in Maryland and Connecticut felt the shock. The blast lobbed seventy-five-millimeter shells as far as Ellis Island in New York Harbor, causing over $20 million worth of damage, most of it in Jersey City, including $1,000,000 worth of shattered windows in the New Jersey-New York metropolitan area. Miraculously, only seven people died in the explosion. In January 1917, a smaller blast in Kingsland again raised the possibility of German action. Then, on October 4, 1918, a spectacular explosion of a munitions storage facility all but leveled Morgan, near South Amboy. The area looked like a war zone, shells rained down miles away, and the shock waves broke windows in Newark. The German government always denied responsibility for any of the New Jersey blasts, but in 1939, after protracted hearings, an international claims commission held the Germans guilty in the Black Tom incident and ordered them to pay reparations. Despite this finding, however, historians are not sure whether the Germans caused these explosions or not.

If President Wilson urged neutrality in 1917, however, New Jersey's governor in 1917 was not so sure. Republican Walter Edge was pro-Allies, and he was convinced that ties of sympathy and business ultimately would bring the United States into the war against the Central Powers (Germany and Austria-Hungary). Indeed, anticipating Wilson's call for a declaration of war by two weeks, the state legislature voted emergency war powers for Governor Edge in early April. He quickly brought the National Guard up to strength, placed Guard units at critical industrial and transport facilities, and, because he counted on a federal call-up of the guard, organized a state militia to replace the guard for local duty. He also selected sites for military bases, on which the national government subsequently built Camp (later Fort) Dix in Wrightstown and Camp Merritt in Tenafly and Dumont. Dix became a major training facility, and Merritt was an embarkation camp.

Wilson was able to maintain neutrality until 1917. From the beginning the Allied strategy was to cripple Germany's war machine and starve its people into submission by imposing a naval blockade on continental Europe. Germany answered with unrestricted submarine warfare, sinking ships of all the Allies and their trade partners. After the *Lusitania* tragedy the Germans suspended this policy for fear that America would enter the war. But by late 1916 the ground war had become a bloody stalemate, and Germany concluded that it had to destroy the Allied means of supply. If it sank enough ships to cut trade links with America quickly, it believed, it could force the war to an end before America could put an effective fighting force in place. Germany resumed submarine attacks in January 1917, and the United States declared war in April.

As Edge expected, Washington quickly federalized the New Jersey National Guard. The era of state regiments marching to the front, however, had passed. The army integrated most of the guardsmen into the United States Twenty-ninth ("Blue and Gray") and Seventy-eighth ("Lightning") Infantry divisions, while a Guard ambulance company went to the Forty-second ("Rainbow") Division. The Twenty-ninth, combining Jerseymen and Southerners, trained at Fort McClellan (named after the general and New Jersey governor) in Alabama; the Seventy-eighth, including mostly men from New Jersey, New York, and Delaware, was organized at Camp Dix. In addition, men from the state naval militia served throughout the fleet. The Selective Service Act, passed in 1917, brought thousands more Jerseymen to the colors in the first truly national draft. Local boards of election served as draft boards, and Edge saw to it that officials received whatever assistance they needed to make the federal conscription machinery function in the Garden State.

By the time the fighting ended in November 1918, New Jersey had raised an estimated 130,000 men. Of these, 72,946 had been conscripted, another 46,960 had volunteered in the guard, army, navy, or marines, and the rest had either been in federal service when the war began or enlisted outside of New Jersey without recording their residence in the state. The poet Joyce Kilmer was one such recruit; a New Jersey native, he enlisted in New York. A German bullet killed him just before the armistice; many more Jerseymen, no matter where they enlisted, never lived that long. The records of the Twenty-ninth and Seventy-eighth divisions told the grim story. Both units arrived in France in the spring and early summer of 1918, and both suffered brutal casualties in the final offensives that forced Germany to sue for peace in November. The Seventy-eighth took over five thousand casualties in October alone, and when the Twenty-ninth demobilized at Camp Dix in May of 1919, it had lost a third of its strength. They had fallen at places like Belfort, Alsace, the Meuse, and other French towns and districts— charnel houses that lacked any of the supposed romance of San Juan Hill.

The New Jersey home front reflected what was in fact a national mobilization. The state became one of the key transportation centers of the war as products from across the nation came to New Jersey for storage and reshipment. In addition to munitions, other industries boomed in response to military demands. Refining operations in Middlesex County produced half of the nation's copper, and shipyards in Camden, Kearny, Elizabeth, Port Newark, and Gloucester supported the building and refitting of thousands of men-of-war and merchant vessels. The young aircraft industry produced engines for the Allied air forces, while even Singer Sewing Machine converted to military production, turning out recoil systems for French artillery pieces. There is every likelihood that New Jersey would have experienced considerable industrial expansion without the stimulus of war, but there is no denying that the economic results of the conflict were dramatic. State industrial output increased almost 300 percent between 1914 and 1919.

The military and other war-related activities also became a highly visible part of New Jersey civilian life. Besides Camps Merritt and Dix, thirty-six other camps or military installations were established or enlarged. Some, like Picatinny Arsenal in Morris County, employed large numbers of civilians, and the combined spending power of the garrisons alone was enough to make the military a significant force in the state economy. Volunteers worked with the larger bases, sponsoring social and

religious activities for the troops, while others collected funds
for overseas relief efforts, the YMCA (which ran activities for
the troops in France), and the Red Cross. There were four
drives for Liberty Loans (the savings bonds of the era) as well,
and New Jerseyans bought millions of dollars' worth of them.
The New Jersey Council of Defense, a civilian advisory group
attached to the governor's office, coordinated much of this
activity, which extended even to encouraging school children to
grow food for the war effort. The state government also raised
food, using prison and mental hospital populations to cultivate
state lands.

The nation attempted to rally public opinion as well, as
national and state government carefully cultivated a hatred of
virtually all things German. Wagnerian opera was simply not
listened to, German shepherd dogs were renamed "Alsatians,"
and sauerkraut became "liberty cabbage." While New Jersey did
not, as some states did, outlaw the teaching of German, there
was still plenty of hostility in the air. German-American citizens
in such heavily ethnic enclaves as Newark suffered occasional
harassment and accusations of disloyalty. In western Morris
County, a fit of patriotism seized the local government, which
changed the name of the German Valley district (a name people
had lived with for some two hundred years) to Long Valley.
Many of the propaganda excesses of the period seem more silly
than sinister in hindsight, but the entire anti-German campaign
offered an ominous early view of the modern government's
ability to manipulate popular attitudes.

Indeed, once unleashed, officially inspired fears were hard
to control and spilled over into a postwar "Red Scare." The
immediate aftermath of the war was less than reassuring. Instead of a new, democratic, stable order in Europe, there was
a legacy of bitterness and turmoil. Various events prompted
concern. In Russia, the Bolshevik takeover in November 1917
destroyed the democratic promise of that former ally's revolution early in the same year.

The Russians had overthrown their repressive czar, Nicholas
II, in March and replaced his regime with a democratic one
headed by Alexander Kerensky. Kerensky, oblivious of the
profound war-weariness of the Russian people, promised new
resolve against the Germans. The Bolsheviks under Vladimir
Lenin knew better and sued for peace after their coup in

November. Bolshevik promises of "peace, land, and bread" were cheered by a variety of American radicals—pacifists, socialists, communists, and others. These same promises frightened many other Americans, who wondered whether the American left also had plans to redistribute land and wealth.

This question was set in a context of domestic labor unrest. Many American workers had prospered during the war. In the effort to produce war materiel, relations between management and labor had improved. Workers had taken home better pay, worked shorter hours, and upgraded their working conditions. Once the war ended, labor-management relations resumed their hostile tone. A wave of layoffs followed the armistice as companies in New Jersey and elsewhere scaled back on military orders, and the rapid demobilization of the armed services only made unemployment worse. Postwar inflation raised prices and erased wage gains. More than four million American workers went on strike in 1919. Many Americans blamed unions for the higher prices and identified union workers as foreign and radical.

Always suspicious of the left anyway, and capitalizing on the fact that war policy had encouraged the public's fears of domestic and foreign enemies, certain federal officials seized the moment. In 1919 and early 1920, Attorney General A. Mitchell Palmer and Assistant Attorney General J. Edgar Hoover, who later became director of the FBI, launched a sweep of domestic political and social dissenters. Hundreds of people were detained illegally, both Americans and aliens. Aliens, including naturalized citizens abruptly deprived of their citizenship, were deported willy-nilly.

New Jersey was not immune to the hysteria. Federal and local officials across the state arrested hundreds of alleged communists, socialists, or radicals of various persuasions, usually on the flimsiest of charges. Agents picked up one Newark man because he "looked like a radical" as he walked down the street.[1] In the New Brunswick area, federal authorities briefly thought they had hit paydirt. Raiding parties seized what they took to be bomb designs and some actual explosives. No luck: the design drawings were for a phonograph and the bombs were bowling balls. In the face of such nonsense the antiradical crusade lost momentum, most of those arrested quickly went free, and the raids ended by 1920. Nonsense or not, however, the postwar Red Scare posed menacing questions about the status of civil liberties in the face of officially inspired hatred. To its credit, the *Newark News* was one of the few papers in the nation to denounce the entire fiasco from the beginning. Fortunately, other aspects of postwar adjustment were more positive. After a slump, the state economy rebounded, providing employment to many returning veterans. Governor Edge encouraged the state to rehire civil servants who had left government jobs to serve in the military, and he sponsored a $12 million bond issue to pay soldiers a bonus (in lieu of other veterans' benefits). The state also appropriated funds for a new home for disabled veterans, replacing an institution founded in 1866 to provide for Civil War veterans. The modern facility opened its doors in 1932 in Menlo Park. Veterans' affairs generally became a significant New Jersey concern. Around the state, veterans' organizations, notably the newly founded American Legion, initiated a long-term drive to secure pensions, medical benefits, educational opportunities, and employment preferences for veterans. The Legion also became involved in a range of activities, ranging from the sponsorship of baseball teams and care for sick and orphaned children to the effort to assure "100-percent Americanism" in the public schools. The Legion quickly became more influential than the GAR had been in its heyday after the Civil War. If the Legion was controversial in some of its positions, its growth and work marked the arrival of organized veterans as a potent social and political force. Indeed, by 1936, the push for a national veterans' bonus measure was so effective that a group of Princeton University students organized a parody group, the Veterans of Future Wars, demanding *pre*payment of bonuses they expected to earn through participation in later conflicts.

As a war "to end war" or "to make the world safe for democracy" (as the Wilson administration had hoped), World War I was a colossal failure. It hardly ended war. Revolution and turmoil wracked Europe in its aftermath, Allied expeditionary forces briefly occupied parts of the Soviet Union, and democracy never stood a chance or took only shallow root in many nations. Even ending the war was difficult, as President Wilson found when he tried, perhaps naively, to temper the vengeful demands of the other victorious Allies. Many Americans were profoundly disappointed with the entire business, and the reaction against involvement in Europe contributed to the Senate's refusal to ratify the Treaty of Versailles or to sanction joining the League of Nations. Later, the Senate held lengthy hearings on charges that American bankers and munitions manufacturers, whose fortunes in French and British loans and arms deals would have evaporated with a German victory, really were behind America's declaration of war. The hearings proved only that some businesses made money from the war—no surprise—but they generated considerable publicity and further contributed to the popular disillusionment with the conflict. The bitter legacy of the postwar period left most Americans suspicious of future foreign entanglements.

Prelude to War

By the late 1930s, the world was moving rapidly toward catastrophe once again. The wounds of World War I had never healed. In Europe, political and economic discord proved fertile ground for totalitarian movements. By the mid-1920s, Benito Mussolini's Fascists* had seized power in Italy, and German Nazis* went delirious with joy when Adolf Hitler came to power in 1933. Lacking the will or ability to present a united front, the rest of Europe watched as the fascist states and their Asian ally, Japan,* rearmed and embarked on policies of naked aggression. In the Far East, Japan attacked China, and then walked out of the League of Nations rather than endure the criticisms of that impotent body. Italy and Germany sent money, guns, and men to the support of Francisco Franco's successful fascist revolt in Spain. With visions of a new Roman Empire, Italy colonized Ethiopia. Most disturbing of all, the Western democracies did little or nothing to stop Germany from reoccupying the Rhineland, annexing Austria, and forcing the cession of important parts of Czechoslovakia. Finally, in September 1939, Hitler's invasion of Poland forced Britain and France to act. Honoring commitments to Poland, they declared war.

Across the Atlantic, an overwhelming majority of Americans wanted none of it. With many Americans disgruntled over the outcome of the First World War, and preoccupied with the Great Depression,* the United States sought to avoid foreign diplomatic entanglements during the 1930s, especially those likely to result in military confrontations. Many political and social leaders held strong isolationist sentiments. President Franklin D. Roosevelt clearly expressed the will of the nation when he declared the country neutral and insisted he would not send American boys to fight in another foreign war.

Yet the United States was not oblivious of the dangers inherent in an Axis* victory, and the sympathies of most Americans lay with Britain, France and, after Hitler struck east in June 1941, with the Soviet Union. Citing defensive needs, Roosevelt accelerated American rearmament, and gradually, because he did not want to provoke an isolationist political reaction, he increased military shipments to the antifascist powers. The fall of France in the spring of 1940 made American assistance even more critical. Despite the strident objections of those who feared that offering military aid would draw the United States into the conflict, the president ultimately agreed to provide the Allies with "all aid short of war"; the United States would be the "Arsenal of Democracy." By 1941, under the Lend-Lease program, millions of tons of American munitions and supplies were reaching British and Soviet forces. Inevitably, relations soured with Germany, and in September 1941 the first prewar shooting incident occurred between a U-boat* and an American destroyer. The role of arsenal of democracy had its risks.

Aid to the Allies, and the American military build-up, depended on a major mobilization of industrial might. New Jersey played a leading role in this critical effort. New orders for military and industrial goods of all kinds revived shops, factories, mines, ports and other facilities that had been idled during the Depression. In northern New Jersey, zinc and iron mines spurred production, and copper refining in Middlesex County resumed its former prominence as the government and other businesses placed huge orders. Munitions development at Picatinny Arsenal added hundreds (later thousands) of workers to the payroll, as did the Hercules and DuPont powder plants. In Paterson, the Wright corporation became one of the largest aircraft engine producers in the world; and orders to various companies established New Jersey as the fourth largest aircraft manufacturing center in the country. The story was the same elsewhere. Production soared in steel, electrical supplies, textiles and rubber products, oil refining, chemicals, drugs and medical supplies, power, agriculture, and communications equipment. Port facilities and transport flourished as well. Once again, New Jersey demonstrated that the key to modern war lay in a prosperous and technologically advanced industrial base.

Shipbuilding deserves special mention in this regard. Participation in any Asian or European war would require the United States to project its power overseas, defend its coasts, and maintain its sea lanes. Thus, much of the military build-up emphasized the navy, and the Garden State did some of its best work in expanding and refitting the fighting and merchant fleets. Federal Shipbuilding and Dry Dock Corporation in Kearny turned out a range of vessels. Between the late 1930s and 1941, the hulls of destroyers, cruisers, transports, and support craft went into the water in record time. Across the state, the yards of New York Shipbuilding in Camden were just as busy. Some of the ships built in Camden before 1941, including the battleship *South Dakota* and the seaplane tender *Curtiss,* made headlines within a few years.

Administration of much of the fleet expansion fell to Acting Secretary of the Navy Charles Edison, Thomas A. Edison's son, who would become governor of New Jersey in 1941. He pressed the building program energetically, and fostered the development of the small but deadly patrol-torpedo (PT) boats that proved their mettle in the Philippines in 1942. Not incidentally, he also decided the name of a new 45,000-ton Iowa-class battleship scheduled for construction in the Philadelphia Navy Yard, the *New Jersey.* Carolyn Edison, the governor's wife, christened her on December 7, 1942, a year to the day after the Japanese attack on Pearl Harbor.

The extent of the economic recovery in New Jersey was remarkable. Defense orders helped Garden State industries put some 433,000 men and women on payrolls by 1939, the highest employment level in twenty years. This figure increased by 50 percent during the following year, while the actual value of payrolls doubled. These trends continued through 1941. The state was experiencing the most rapid period of industrial expansion in history. The battle against the Axis lay ahead, but New Jersey had won the war against the Depression.

Military preparedness, however, proceeded more cautiously through 1940. An industrial build-up—with its attendant prosperity—was one thing; but the public was still skittish about a troop call-up. However, circumstances changed in June 1940: France and the Low Countries (Belgium, Luxembourg, and the Netherlands) fell, and the beaten British army lost most of its equipment when it evacuated the French port of Dunkirk. As a precaution, the U.S. Army called up the National Guard for training; most of the New Jersey outfits reported to Fort Dix. It was not much of a military display. The states had paid little attention to the guard (at least as a force that might have to fight a war) during the 1930s, and most units were in sorry shape. Equipment was in such short supply that some outfits drilled with broomsticks, and it quickly became evident that even a second-rate panzer* division would have pulverized any American unit in the field. But the exercise at least tested mobilization machinery, pointed out organizational and equipment weaknesses, and served notice on the public that matters were taking a serious turn. In the fall of 1940, President Roosevelt instituted America's first peace-time draft. It was a courageous step, coming as it did in the middle of a hotly contested presidential election in whch peace had become a key issue. But there was little serious protest in New Jersey (which FDR carried in the election), and the first conscripts from the state reported for basic training early in 1941. Some of them did not really believe they would end up in a shooting war.

They were wrong. On the morning of December 7, 1941, carrier-based Japanese aircraft struck the main battle line of the navy's Pacific fleet at Pearl Harbor, Hawaii. It was a brilliant stroke, and with minimal losses (twenty-nine planes, one large submarine and five midget subs) they sank or damaged eighteen American ships, including eight battleships. They also destroyed or hit over three hundred planes and vital shore installations, killed 2,403 people and wounded another 1,178. Outraged, Congress declared war the next day. Within the week, after a declaration of war on the United States by Hitler, the nation entered the European struggle as well. The war Americans had dreaded for more than two years was upon them.

Hostilities evoked a variety of responses from New Jerseyans. For some, the war presented an immediate fight for survival. Tom Mahoney was one of these. He and his brother had worked on a farm in Bergen County until early 1941, when they had both enlisted in the navy. After training, the Mahoney brothers joined the crew of a seaplane tender, the Camden-built USS

Curtiss, and sailed with her to Pearl Harbor in the late spring. Tom Mahoney enjoyed Hawaii, and on December 7 he looked forward to a day off. He never got it. Hearing the sound of bombs, and then the alarm for general quarters, he reported to a *Curtiss* damage-control party. The Japanese hit the ship hard. A bomb killed twenty men and set raging fires, while a crippled attacking aircraft crashed aboard. Fighting the fires, Mahoney pushed pieces of the downed plane over the side and then bagged the pilot's body. That evening, with the *Curtiss* safe, he stood on deck and spoke to a sailor covered with oil. Only when the man answered did Tom recognize him as his brother.

If the Mahoney brothers lived to fight another day, however, three others from New Jersey did not. Killed in action—the state's first fatalities of the war—were sergeants G. R. Schnersahl of Bloomfield and Ralph Alois of Paterson, and Private Louis Schleifer of Newark. Thousands more would follow them before the guns fell silent.

USS **Curtiss.** *Built in the Camden yards of the New York Shipbuilding Company shortly before World War II, the Curtiss was a seaplane tender— that is, a ship designed to service the Navy's seaplanes, many of which played important reconnaissance and communications roles. The Curtiss was hit hard in the Japanese attack on Pearl Harbor on December 7, 1941, but served throughout the rest of the war. U.S. NAVY PHOTOGRAPH.*

Back home, the shock of December 7 was profound. Families gathered around radios (World War II was the first war reported over the air waves) waiting for news, while across the state thousands of men mobbed recruiting stations the next morning. Whatever else they did, the Japanese killed off any American reluctance to fight. Taking no chances against a Pearl Harbor at home, the state's larger cities quickly instituted emergency measures. Newark, Bayonne, and Jersey City, for example, called up all fire and police forces, placed guards at key industrial and communications sites, including the Lincoln and Holland tunnels, and established air-raid warning systems. In Newark, Bamberger's (now Macy's) Department Store quickly put civil defense uniforms on the shelves, while Kresge's reported brisk sales of blackout coverings for windows. In hindsight, many of these precautions appear overly dramatic. The possibility of a Japanese or German raid on, say, Bayonne, was far-fetched. But in the last days of 1941, who knew? In fact, a Gallup Poll in late December found 45 percent of East Coast residents convinced that enemy attacks would hit their cities.

There were also some concerns over domestic subversion. The German-American Bund had attracted suspicion since the 1930s. Its members, mostly Germans from the old country or their families, generally shared a pride in the resurgent Germany without any inherent disloyalty to the United States. But there were virulent Nazis in the Bund as well, and chants of *"Sieg Heil!"* anti-semitic slogans, and marching columns of brown-shirts shaped the group's public image. (In addition to the Bund, a few pro-Facist Italian-Americans organized the "Silver Shirts." They sometimes cooperated with the Bund, although they were of limited influence.) The Bund ran three camps in New Jersey—a youth facility near Griggstown, Camp Nordland, near Andover, and Camp Bergwald, near Bloomingdale. The American Legion, Jewish war veterans, and other groups occasionally got into fistfights with Bundists, and law enforcement officers near the Bund camps kept tabs on members and later supplied information to weed Bund members out of defense-related jobs. In the heated atmosphere after Pearl Harbor, federal and local officials swept up prominent Bund leaders, making arrests that played fast and loose with the Constitution and rounding up innocent people with genuine Bundists. In the end, federal trials in Newark convicted only nine men under enemy-agent or espionage-and-sedition laws. The treatment of the Bund underlined the tensions between genuine national security concerns and a regard for civil liberties in time of war. In any case, the country was taking no chances with a group whose loyalty was so much in doubt.

The matter of the Bund also touched on coastal defense. Early in the war, U-boats landed several parties of saboteurs at locations from Florida to New England. Most of a group that came ashore on Long Island were former Bundists. New Jersey's long coastline was clearly vulnerable to such landings, and military and civil authorities quickly took defensive measures. The Coast Guard, which already had stations along the seashore, posted guards at major ports and established regular foot patrols on the beaches. These "beach pounders," with their dogs, became regular features of life at the shore during the war years. Military aircraft, augmented by the Civil Air Patrol, flew scouting missions over coastal waters, and silo-like towers went up at key points along the beaches. At Fort Hancock on Sandy Hook, and at Cape May Point, the army improved existing artillery positions or installed new ones to defend approaches to the New York area ports and to Delaware Bay and Philadelphia.

This activity had genuine urgency, for in early 1942 New Jersey came as close as it ever did to front-line status. In a move that threw the navy off balance, the Germans moved their U-boats into the western Atlantic and launched a determined assault on shipping off America's ports and coasts. The inland waterway, much of which threaded its course behind New Jersey's barrier islands, afforded protection to many craft, but those in the open sea were vulnerable. From the Gulf Coast to New England, the U-boats had a field day. Oil and wreckage washed ashore with alarming frequency along New Jersey beaches, and several times merchantmen burned and went down within sight of the beach. While the navy regrouped to drive off the Nazi raiders, an astonishing battle developed on the home front in the spring of 1942. Fearing the loss of the tourist trade, an alarming number of East Coast seashore businesses, including many in New Jersey, refused to participate in blackout procedures. As a result, U-boat commanders patrolling at night found, to their delight, Allied ships silhouetted against lights

U.S. Navy Blimp. *During World War II, blimps became a familiar part of the New Jersey seashore. Operating out of the Navy air station at Lakehurst, they patrolled coastal waters looking for German U-boats or hostile activities. The blimps continued their patrols into the 1960s.* COURTESY THE NEW JERSEY HISTORICAL SOCIETY.

ashore—rather like targets in a shooting gallery. Enraged federal officials had to go to court to enforce the blackout, but in the meantime, ships and lives were hostage to the thirst for tourist dollars. As historian Samuel Eliot Morrison noted with disgust, it was one of "the most reprehensible" home-front incidents of the war.[2]

While New Jersey sorted out the events of late 1941 and early 1942, the war effort shifted into high gear. Already extremely productive, the state's industrial base performed wonders. Shifts worked around the clock in all key industries, and Garden State workers ultimately filled a sixteenth of all American orders for war materiel and manufactures. By the end of the war, almost a million men and women in war-related industries filled $12 billion in contracts, producing everything from battleships and aircraft carriers to the engines that powered James Doolittle's raiders over Tokyo in 1942 and the *Enola Gay*, bearing the atomic bomb, over Hiroshima in 1945. Light industry and small businesses played their roles as well, turning out parts for assembly in heavier plants. Indeed, New Jersey had so many small parts manufacturers that some industrial leaders began referring to it as the "components state."

The "training" or "staging state" would have fit as well. Military posts proliferated as the army and navy built depots, air and naval stations, communications centers, and coastal positions. A number of bases attained special importance. Fort Dix quickly became one of the largest basic training centers in the nation. By 1945, some 1.3 million draftees had passed through the post. In Edison and Piscataway townships, Camp Kilmer appeared on what had been farm land in 1942, becoming the army's main embarkation facility. Kilmer sent 2 million men to the European fronts at a rate of a hundred thousand per month. Not only men embarked. Amid some of the tightest security in the armed forces, personnel at the Earle Naval Ammunition Depot in Monmouth County shipped almost 130,000 tons of explosives each month to Allied fleets in the Atlantic. At any given time, the depot held one of the largest concentrations of munitions in the world—enough, as one estimate put it, "to blow all of New Jersey and New York City off the map."[3] These facilities were vital cogs in the vast logistical machinery of the war effort, and their operations illustrated the extent to which warfare had become dependent on the management skills required for moving masses of men and materiel.

Scientific advances were also crucial to victory. Scientists and engineers in industry and academia pursued countless basic and applied research projects with military applications. At Rutgers University, for example, different laboratories worked on efforts as varied as advanced electronics, trauma treatment techniques, and improved methods for preserving the finish, and thus the speed and performance, of the hulls of Navy ships. Albert Einstein was a member of the Institute for Advanced Study in Princeton when he wrote his famous letter to President Roosevelt warning of the dangerous potential of atomic weapons. Other members of the Institute, notably Professor Hugh

Scott Taylor, carried out some of the key heavy-water experiments that helped enable the nation to build the A-bomb. Professor J. Robert Oppenheimer, who headed the project to build the bomb in the New Mexico desert, became director of the Institute for Advanced Study after the war. In Bloomfield, Westinghouse scientists, using data from a discovery in company laboratories dating from 1922, began large-scale production of uranium for the atomic bomb project. The technical demands of modern warfare clearly accelerated the growth of ties between government, corporate, and academic research and development efforts. These ties, established amid intense controversy over their nature and propriety, have endured to the present day.

The requirements of science and industry made special demands on education. The nation's schools were a crucial factor in providing the technical and management skills necessary to support increasingly sophisticated war production and research operations. Consequently, New Jersey educational institutions also became part of the mobilization effort. At Rutgers, for example, the curriculum quickly adjusted to military-industrial needs as engineering, management, and scientific courses largely replaced the traditional liberal arts. The need for skilled workers kept the state's vocational schools open twenty-four hours a day, and the public schools added new courses or increased existing emphases on mathematics, radio operations, physical education, citizenship, electricity, and aeronautics. In 1941 the New Jersey Department of Public Instruction began an important collaborative project with the federal Office of Production Management. Called the New Jersey Plan, the effort used schools and other state facilities, as well as private plants, to train twenty thousand industrial supervisors per year. The project worked so well that other states adopted it, helping to assure the relatively smooth functioning of the astonishingly complex mechanisms of the home front.

The war effort, civilian and military, touched almost all aspects of daily life. There were, of course, the obvious signs of war—mass conscription and burgeoning industrial production—but there were also less dramatic reminders that government had drafted the services of virtually all levels of society. School children, for example, learned how to use ration and savings stamps, assisted with scrap-metal salvage drives, and planted victory gardens. Traditional race relations also felt the impact of war. Federal directives made racial discrimination illegal in hiring for war-contract jobs, and thousands of blacks found work in New Jersey factories. More moved into the state, primarily from the South, continuing a trend that had begun during World War I. South Jersey saw an influx of Bahamian and Jamaican farm workers, who immigrated with federal assistance to fill a wartime labor shortage in agriculture. The war clearly increased black economic participation in New Jersey life and fueled desires for greater social and political participation as well. The state was set for significant advances in civil rights legislation in the immediate postwar years.

The war also drew women more deeply into the economic life of the state. They stepped onto assembly lines and into manufacturing and management jobs in unprecedented numbers, replacing husbands and sons who had entered the armed forces. As early as 1940, a third of New Jersey women over fourteen years old had jobs outside the home. "Rosie the Riveter" was a reality in many New Jersey aircraft plants, and by 1942, fully 76 percent of all Bell Telephone employees were women. After the war, there was a backlash against women in the industrial workplace, but the war years had raised modern expectations of social and economic participation among women. Even in the face of stiff opposition, there could be no turning back the clock.

On Duty

While the New Jersey home front turned out the machines of war, the state's sons and daughters carried the battle to the Axis powers. Some 560,500 state residents served in the armed services, about 346,000 of them as draftees. For the first time, a substantial number of women wore the unform. About ten thousand New Jersey women enlisted in the WAVES (Navy), WACS (Army), and other services, further illustrating the extent of the national mobilization. These men and women served on every fighting front, on the high seas, and across the skies. Before the shooting stopped, more than thirteen thousand had died abroad or in the service at home; seventeen won the Congressional Medal of Honor for gallantry under fire (and ten of these died doing so). The stories of these men and women are legion and too varied to summarize, and historians are only beginning to examine their experiences in detail. Two examples will have to do here.

The Quiet Marine

Marine Sergeant John Basilone of Raritan was one of New Jersey's best-known soldiers. The son of immigrants from Italy, he won the Congressional Medal of Honor for gallantry during the brutal fighting against the Japanese on Guadalcanal in 1942. Recalled from active duty, the Marine hero was sent on tour selling war bonds. Basilone, a shy man, disliked the limelight and asked to return to his unit. He did, and he never saw New

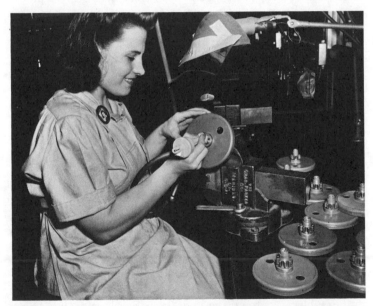

Woman at work in the Propeller Division, Curtiss-Wright Corporation, Caldwell, April 1942. The corporation released this photo to the press with a caption describing her as "one of many women now reporting for work for the first time" as "part of the all-out program for Victory through Production." COURTESY THE NEW JERSEY PICTURE COLLECTION, NEWARK PUBLIC LIBRARY.

Jersey again. In February 1945, Sergeant Basilone died—one
of more than five thousand American combat deaths—in the
blistering battle for the island of Iwo Jima. A statue of the
gallant Marine stands in Raritan.

Women in Uniform
    Commander Joy Bright Hancock, who came from the shore
community of Wildwood, had enlisted in the Navy during World
War I, one of the first handful of American women sailors. As
a civilian working for naval agencies after the war, she became
something of an authority on naval aviation as well as an
advocate for women in the armed forces. With the coming of
war in 1941, she became a ranking WAVE, pushing hard to
expand the roles open to women in uniform. Hancock gained
considerable recognition for her efforts to make the WAVES
an effective force, and especially for her success in helping to
persuade the navy to train women in aircraft maintenance and
other skills previously reserved for men. Her efforts made it
possible for women to contribute to the military to an extent
never permitted (or even imagined) before, and did as much
as anyone to clear the way for women to pursue naval careers
in the post-war years. With the end of the war, Hancock received a hero's welcome when she came home to Wildwood—
perhaps one of the first celebrations of its kind for any American woman.

A Different Kind of Struggle
    The American military was still legally segregated during
World War II. Black soldiers and sailors served in all-black
outfits. The navy assigned Joseph Small (who later settled in
Somerset) to a segregated unit loading munitions ships in Port
Chicago Naval Station in California. On July 17, 1944, a tremen-
dous explosion, almost surely the result of unsafe working
conditions and violations of munitions-handling procedures,
leveled much of the yard and killed two hundred men, most
of them black ammunition handlers. Small survived, helped
rescue the wounded, and got loading operations moving again.
Yet when officers continued to ignore safety precautions, he
found himself the impromptu leader of a black sailors' protest.
He and forty-nine other sailors were court-martialed for their
trouble, and they served sixteen months at hard labor. The case,

however, had taken on racial overtones, and the NAACP rallied to Small's defense. The association's special counsel (later Supreme Court Justice) Thurgood Marshall helped lead a legal fight that ultimately returned Small and his comrades to the fleet. The case illustrated the inequities inherent in racially segregating the armed forces—and showed that the fight against the Axis would mean little for many citizens if it left legal discrimination intact at home. Small's difficult stand was yet another sign that the war had stirred the winds of social change.

Death at Sea
Ships have lives as well as the people who build and sail them. One of the most impressive vessels to come out of a New Jersey yard was the light cruiser USS *Atlanta*. Begun at Federal Ship-building in Kearny in 1940, *Atlanta* was christened two weeks after Pearl Harbor by Margaret Mitchell, author of *Gone With the Wind*. In June 1942, the new cruiser fought in the epic Battle of Midway. During the summer and fall she took an active part in operations around Guadalcanal, where she made her greatest fight. On the night of November 12–13, under orders from Elizabeth-born Admiral William Halsey, she steamed out as part of an outnumbered task force to meet a massive enemy naval assault. Opening fire at contact, the *Atlanta* quickly sent a destroyer to the bottom and then helped finish off a cruiser. But the Japanese also had the range. Torpedoed and shelled repeatedly, the New Jersey-built ship stayed in the fight until flooding engine rooms drove her ashore. She finally went down—half a world away from her Kearny birthplace—a third of her crew dead or wounded. Yet the desperate struggle had stopped the more powerful enemy force, and the threat to the embattled Americans on Guadalcanal ultimately passed. The *Atlanta* and her crew had gone down in a winning fight against deadly odds.

Enola Gay
By the summer of 1945 the war was entering its final bloody phase. Germany had surrendered to the Allies in May, and in battle after battle, American assaults had driven the Japanese back across the Pacific. Desperate engagements had all but wiped out the Imperial fleet, and devastating air raids began gutting Japan's cities. Cautiously, figures around the Emperor

sought a way out of the war, but hard-liners insisted on fighting to the end. Grimly, American planners prepared to invade the home islands of Japan in the late autumn of 1945, expecting to suffer and to inflict hundreds of thousands of casualties. But the invasion fleet never sailed. On August 6, a B-29 Superfortress bomber, with engines of a type built by the thousands in New Jersey, flew from the island of Tinian toward the city of Hiroshima, Japan. Colonel Paul Tibbets commanded the aircraft, *Enola Gay;* Captain Robert A. Lewis, of Ridgefield Park, flew as copilot. Over the city, they dropped an atomic bomb of some twenty kilotons*—not much by today's megaton* standards, but enough to raze the ancient city and to snuff out some eighty thousand lives (although estimates of the deaths vary widely). The age of atomic warfare, the ultimate combination of war, science, and industry, had begun. Three days later, another atomic blast incinerated Nagasaki, and on August 14 Japan decided to surrender. World War II had ended, but a mushroom cloud hung over the peace.

CHAPTER SEVEN

Postwar New Jersey

The end of World War II left the United States with the most powerful military machine in recorded history. Swiftly, however, the victorious armed forces demoblized, and by late 1946 the standing army, navy, and air units (which became the air force as part of the National Security Act of 1947) were mere shadows of the legions that had brought the Axis powers to their knees. Millions of men and women returned to civilian life, even as the government was canceling billions of dollars in war contracts and factories were laying off hundreds of thousands of workers. By October 1945 more than three hundred thousand New Jersey wage earners, many of them women, had lost their jobs. Many economists feared a painful economic readjustment to peace at best—at worst, a return to depression.

These dire predictions never materialized. Rather, in New Jersey as in much of the nation, the postwar years saw a booming economy and sweeping social changes. Even in 1945, employment never fell to 1939 levels, and it then climbed again to record heights as thousands of veterans began families, stimulating markets for housing, automobiles, appliances, clothing, and a range of other consumer goods. Indeed, as the historian John T. Cunningham has noted, one of the most visible aspects of the postwar boom was the fact that many appliance and car salesmen got rich. The federal government subsidized a great deal of this prosperity through veterans' mortgages, which allowed young servicemen to acquire homes on attractive terms. The construction industry surged, and enormous tracts of the Garden State became suburbs during the late 1940s and early 1950s. Widespread ownership of automobiles allowed developers to build farther from the old population centers, which in turn spurred highway construction. The face of New Jersey changed forever after the war.

Education changed as well. One of the most important federal benefits offered veterans was the GI Bill of Rights, which made higher education possible for tens of thousands of New Jersey's former soldiers and sailors. The influx of veterans taxed the facilities of the state's colleges and universities to the limit. Rutgers, for example, had to house students at nearby Camp Kilmer and at Raritan Arsenal while trying to build new dormitory space as quickly as possible. At Newark State Teachers College, returning servicemen found themselves in a novel situation: they were the first large group of male students to attend what had been primarily a woman's college. They quickly and cheerfully got used to it. In retrospect, the era of the GI student seems "a period of peculiar vitality" on campus.[1] The veterans were motivated, serious, and largely successful students. Their performance was a stunning demonstration of the fact that a high proportion of the public could benefit from higher education. Moreover, having succeeded themselves, graduating veterans expected similar educational opportunities for their children. In fact, the GI Bill probably did as much as anything in history to raise expectations that higher education ought to be open to the broad masses of the American people.

The war's impact on elementary and secondary education was, if anything, even more pronounced. The birth rate soared as veterans established families, and this sudden "growth spurt" was "followed by yearly population increases that were unmatched in the nation's history."[2] New Jersey's population increased by some 680,000 people between 1940 and 1950 (to 4,835,329), with most of the change coming after 1945. This "baby boom" generation overwhelmed the public school system in a decade. Localities poured hundreds of millions of dollars into school construction in the 1950s and early 1960s, and the state colleges graduated thousands of teachers—many of them veterans—to staff the new classrooms. In the early and mid-1960s, the "war babies" swamped the state's colleges and universities, and thousands of high school graduates pursued their postsecondary studies out of state for want of space at home. Quite clearly, educating the baby boomers was a challenge unique in the history of education.

There were other reminders of the recent conflict as well. The war had devastated Europe, decimating and uprooting entire populations. In the late 1940s and early 1950s, some of the survivors of these torturous years and their aftermath began to find their way to America, and New Jersey became host to a significant number of refugees. Many of these were Jewish victims of the Holocaust, most of whom had lost their families and neighbors in the Nazi death camps. They came to the Garden State with the support of Jewish and other relief agencies, often arriving virtually penniless. Slowly, they rebuilt lives that the European calamity had destroyed, and many of them made vital contributions to the life of the state. Their presence reminds others forcefully of what happened in the Nazi death camps. In the mid-1950s still more displaced victims of oppression arrived. When the Soviet Union crushed a Hungarian revolt against a Soviet-imposed postwar regime, thousands of Hungarians fled their homeland. Attracted in part by the large Hungarian minority in central New Jersey (especially in and around New Brunswick), many of the Hungarian refugees eventually settled in the state, some after a temporary stay in facilities at Camp Kilmer. New Jersey always had been ethnically and culturally diverse, and the tragic turmoil in Europe added a new dimension to the social composition of the Garden State.

Events in the postwar years also had a profound effect on the growing civil rights movement. The war had crystalized sentiments against racial discrimination, and the state constitution of 1947 reflected these new attitudes. The local military was among the first of the state's institutions to reflect the changing times. Acting under the new state charter, Governor Alfred E. Driscoll ordered the integration of the previously segregated New Jersey National Guard. Driscoll's action was a first. Federal regulations had allowed the states to maintain their guard units according to "local custom," which frequently meant segregated outfits. Following New Jersey's lead, other states also desegregated their guards, and in 1948 President Harry S Truman ordered an end to discrimination in the national armed forces. Consequently, when Americans were sent to fight in Korea in 1950, blacks and whites served in the same combat outfits for the first time.

Even as New Jersey adjusted to demographic and other social changes, matters of immediate military concern regained the public eye. The Berlin Crisis of 1947 and the bitter and prolonged Korean War were grim reminders that the Cold War, which had alienated the Soviet Union from its wartime western allies, could turn hot. Indeed, these fears took on a new dimension when the first Soviet atomic weapons tests broke the American nuclear monopoly in 1949. The new weapons technology, and the destructive potential of long-range aircraft and (by the later 1950s) missiles, diminished as never before the security Americans felt behind the vast Atlantic and Pacific barriers.

New Jersey both witnessed and participated in the military activities related to the Cold War. While many military bases cut back their operations or closed in the aftermath of World War II, the state remained home to important installations. With the return of conscription in 1948, Fort Dix again became one of the largest basic training posts, while adjacent McGuire Air Force Base became the largest military airport in the world. Fort Monmouth became one of the army's most productive research and development commands. Navy blimps based at Lakehurst Naval Air Station patrolled coastal areas, while the ammunition depot at Earle eventually added atomic weapons to its lethal inventory (a fact which, as a matter of policy, military authorities have never confirmed). Picatinny Arsenal maintained its role as a significant weapons research and development command, and Fort Hancock on Sandy Hook became the site of one of the country's earliest operational air-defense missile positions. BOMARC missiles (early versions of the modern cruise missiles*), armed with nuclear warheads* and intended for strategic attack missions, sat on launchers at McGuire. It was all indicative of the fact that the postwar era was an uneasy time, and that military technology could now hurl untold destruction between continents.

The Korean War

Few developments posed a greater threat to the stability of the postwar world than the conflict in Korea. President Harry S. Truman ordered American forces into action when communist North Korea invaded South Korea in June 1950. While the ensuing war officially pitted the United Nations (which voted to defend South Korea) against the North, and later Red China, the bulk of the U.N. troops came from the United States. Many of these soldiers were reservists brought back to active duty, and they fought a grueling and lonely war. While the conflict was a deadly business for those on the firing line and a source of anxiety for their loved ones, few Americans were enthusiastic about the struggle. For many, Korea seemed far from vital to American security. Besides, the United States of the late 1940s and early 1950s was preoccupied with its booming postwar economy and a changing society. The last thing Americans wanted was another war.

Troops from New Jersey were involved from the start. Some went into action with contingents hurriedly assembled from units occupying Japan. They were ill-trained and poorly equipped—their antitank rockets, for example, often bounced harmlessly off North Korea's Russian-built armor—and the invading communists inflicted terrible punishment. It was a horror for the men involved. One infantryman from Newark recalled running out of ammunition and watching helplessly as a communist soldier shot him at close range. Only the timely arrival of a U.S. tank saved the wounded GI from certain death. First Lieutenant Samuel Coursen of Madison was not so lucky.

Having won the Bronze and Silver Stars for gallantry, he fell on October 12, 1950; Coursen won a posthumous Medal of Honor during the United Nations counterattack that broke the back of the North Korean army.

The fortunes of war ebbed and flowed until mid-1950. By then, the battle had become a grinding stalemate on a line just north of the Thirty-Eighth Parallel, the border between North and South Korea. The fighting ended only after the United Nations, including the United States, accepted less than victory—they would not drive the communists from power in the North—and North Korea tacitly agreed to let the South alone. It had been a costly three years: America lost over 33,600 dead and suffered more than 103,000 wounded. China and North Korea endured enormously higher casualties. The truce has stood to this day, marred by occasional violence, and both sides maintain large troop concentrations along a demilitarized zone that spans the width of the Korean peninsula.

In addition to the Korean War, other events also revealed the anxieties of the period. Among the most serious and bizarre incidents was Senator Joseph McCarthy's hunt for communists at Fort Monmouth. He found no subversives, but while an amazed public followed the course of his witch-hunt, he ruined the careers of a number of blameless individuals, created an atmosphere of mistrust and suspicion, and thoroughly disrupted the operations of several of the important and sophisticated projects at the fort. Probably no Russian agent could have done more damage.

Civil Defense concerns also became commonplace. Conceding that New Jersey would probably be hit in another conflict, Civil Defense planners worked out a system of public air raid shelters, supply depots, and warning signals. In the 1950s, school children crouched under their desks or out in the school corridors (the wisdom changed from year to year about the best place to hide) in air raid drills. Along with others across the nation, some New Jersey families built fallout shelters (which a number of local companies sold in prefabricated form) or put away food and other emergency items in their basements. Even while taking part in such activities, however, the public generally conceded that survivors of an atomic attack would face only the bleakest of prospects upon emerging from their shelters. Still, as incidents such as the Cuban missile crisis of 1962 fed anxieties over nuclear confrontation, officials at various levels continued to ponder how society might pick up whatever pieces were left if the worst happened. If nothing else, such thinking at last took into account the fact that a new war would completely obliterate distinctions between the home and fighting fronts.

While this was a horrifying prospect, from a strictly military point of view there was a perverse logic to it. New Jersey industry, with its gigantic work force, was an integral part of the complex technical, research, and manufacturing base that supported the American military. Thousands of civilians worked at Fort Dix, Picatinny, Earle, Lakehurst, McGuire, and other bases, and were as critical to the military's ability to fight as those who served in uniform. This being the case, who, strictly speaking, was really a soldier? Who a civilian? Who was a legitimate target? The questions raised by Union general William T. Sherman's march to the sea during the Civil War now came home with a vengeance.

Still, few New Jersey residents questioned the wisdom of the military's vastly larger presence in postwar society. The Cold War seemed to justify a major military establishment, while, at least after the end of the Korean conflict, the lack of a shooting incident eased fears of a major confrontation with the Soviets. Besides, the economic benefits of the armed forces were, for most New Jerseyans, undeniable. Defense-related industries and military payrolls had an enormous influence on the regional economy, a fact which proved telling even after attitudes toward the military changed during the Vietnam War. During the early 1970s, for example, when the Pentagon considered closing or seriously cutting operations at certain installations—notably Picatinny Arsenal and Fort Dix—even the most liberal and antiwar members of the New Jersey congressional delegation reacted angrily. Congressmen who opposed the war recognized that military installations provided their constituents with many jobs. At any rate, Americans had never drifted so far from their traditional skepticism about large military establishments in time of peace.

Vietnam and After

Whatever else it did, the war in Vietnam prompted a painful and far-reaching reexamination of the military's role in American life. It was an experience that went well beyond the disputes over involvement in the war itself, although the disappointments, passions, and questions loosed by the errand into Southeast Asia clearly sharpened the debate.

Like the rest of the nation, New Jersey residents generally accepted early explanations of why the United States had chosen to intervene in South Vietnam (and this book is not the place to examine them). However, by the late 1960s, public sentiment had begun to turn against the conflict. As the fighting dragged on, no clear statement of American objectives or policy ever emerged. Too frequently, the public caught the government lying about the conduct of the war, and it became abundantly clear that the South Vietnamese government had only a dubious claim on the loyalty of its people. By the early 1970s, while most Americans continued to hope for a favorable resolution of the conflict, polls showed that some 40 percent of the nation opposed the war. While there is little quantitative evidence for comparative purposes, that 40 percent may have represented an opposition larger than anything that confronted Abraham Lincoln during the Civil War.

New Jersey reflected the growing tide of dismay. In Washington, the state's congressional delegation divided sharply over the question, with Republican Senator Clifford Case emerging as a cautious but articulate advocate of disengagement. Campus protests became frequent, with criticism of the war peaking first at Rutgers University in New Brunswick. Protest reached a crescendo with the 1970 invasion of Cambodia, and major student demonstrations rocked not only Rutgers, but Princeton and many other state and private colleges. Protest marchers paraded in front of the Army induction center in Newark and at Fort Dix, and speakers denounced the war at forums across the state. For the first time in decades, people challenged the ethics of defense-related research in state colleges and universities, questioned the legitimacy of the draft, and charged that society itself had become militarized. At their height, antiwar activities rivaled those of New Jersey protests against the Civil War in the 1860s.

The arguments for and against the war should not be taken at face value. They were often the stuff of polemic and partisanship, and neither side ever established a monopoly on virtue—although both claimed it on occasion.

Proponents never could explain the failure of the world's greatest military power to conclude the war satisfactorily. In the face of a large domestic minority that opposed the conflict, and of North Vietnamese willingness to absorb enormous casualties, successive presidents simply could not marshall the popular and political consensus necessary to force a military decision. Nor could "hawks" persuade many of their fellow citizens that support of the South Vietnamese government was justified or that the United States was not simply carrying on a colonialist war against legitimate claims of Vietnamese nationalism.

Most of the war's opponents ignored the genuine anticommunist sentiment in South Vietnam and seemed oblivious

Operation RAW, Jockey Hollow, 1970. Looking like an infantry patrol in Vietnam, these "troops" were actually members of Vietnam Veterans Against the War. The antiwar movement was highly visible by 1970, when the veterans' protest group mounted Operation RAW (Rapid American Withdrawal). Participants "patrolled" through New Jersey towns in an effort to explain their opposition to the conflict in Southeast Asia. The road in Jockey Hollow, outside Morristown, was on a route traveled by Continental Army troops almost two centuries earlier. PHOTO BY TONY VELEZ, COURTESY THE PHOTOGRAPHER.

of the long-term threat their attacks presented to the integrity of the nation's military. Most supporters of the war ignored the damage done by alienating a large portion of the population and refused to acknowledge that many protesters were trying to prevent their country from pursuing a policy they found morally reprehensible.

Neither side conceded any validity to the other's argument, and both sides tended to oversimplify the issues. Hawks overlooked the nastier aspects of the South Vietnamese government; they also questioned the patriotism of the doves instead of addressing their arguments. Doves downplayed the brutality of the North Vietnamese regime while accusing the hawks of supporting South Vietnamese atrocities. Both sides lapsed often into self-righteousness and occasionally bullied their opponents.

There was also the matter of the draft, which was grossly inequitable. A system of deferments allowed thousands of college students, certain professional and occupational groups, and members of National Guard and military reserve units to avoid duty. The majority of all of these groups were white and middle-class, as were those who had the resources to flee to Canada or elsewhere to escape conscription. The burdens of combat therefore fell disproportionately on the poor and on minorities. In fact, when the National Guard moved into Newark to put down the major racial disturbances of 1967, this fact came home bluntly. Distressed black residents of the burning city pointed out, with considerable justice, that the guard was mostly white, with many members who had joined to dodge the draft. Black youths were much more likely to face induction into the regular armed forces. When deferments came under fire in the later 1960s and the white middle class did face a wider draft, opposition to the war stiffened. The militancy of the protest movement fell off considerably after President Richard Nixon replaced mass conscription with a lottery system—the first step toward the current all-volunteer armed services—that called on far fewer men. This is hardly to argue that tens of thousands did not oppose the draft (and the war) out of genuine conviction, but neither could some draft resisters avoid serious charges of self-interest and moral ambiguity.

All of this went on while American soldiers, sailors, marines, airmen, and support troops fought their frustrating war. To their everlasting credit, the vast majority of them did their duty with steadfastness and bravery, even as their government failed to define their mission clearly, as protests grew at home, and as morale and, too often, discipline crumbled. More than 55,000 Americans died before the United States pulled out of the devastated country in 1973 (South Vietnam finally collapsed in 1975). Tens of thousands more were wounded and another two thousand or so were listed as missing in action (including sixty-three from New Jersey). Beyond those were the veterans scarred emotionally by their experience. Unlike previous wars, Vietnam brought no victory parades, and the unpopularity of the war often, unfairly, clung to the men who had fought it. Readjustment was frequently a difficult matter as both veterans and the country learned to cope with the legacy of America's most confusing conflict. The healing took some time, as most Americans preferred not to deal with the aftermath of this war; in fact, they seemed more than willing to put the entire business out of their minds as quickly as possible.

Like other states, New Jersey tried to ease the passage of its veterans back to civilian life. To supplement the GI Bill, and to assist veterans in getting the most from their federal benefits, most New Jersey colleges and universities established veterans' affairs offices. Kean College in Union started the first program in 1971. The state civil service, as it did after World War II, maintained a veterans' preference policy in hiring for many government positions. Many returning troops were experiencing health, emotional, employment, and related problems, and various social service agencies started special counseling programs to assist them. All of these efforts, however, worked mostly at the margins of the veteran population. Generally, as they always had, servicemen returned unsung to families, jobs, and other pursuits on their own. Time would do more than veterans' programs to heal the wounds of Vietnam, and it was not until the early 1980s that the public was ready to applaud these men and women for their service.

Time dealt with other problems as well. As immediate concerns with the war faded, so did many of the animosities born of them. In particular, civilian-military relations normalized again. Public opinion polls indicated rising confidence in the armed forces—confidence far beyond that accorded elected officials. With regard to what had happened in Vietnam, there was something to this. Even some of the most vociferous critics of the war recognized that the military was following civilian orders and policies in Southeast Asia. If there was (and is) fierce debate over the ways in which the army, navy, and air force actually fought the war, no one has made a fully convincing case that the armed services manuevered to get the country into it in the first place. On many New Jersey campuses, ROTC programs, which had come under heavy fire during the war years, made modest comebacks, and activities were also revived at military reserve and National Guard centers throughout the state. New Jerseyans overwhelmingly supported Ronald Reagan

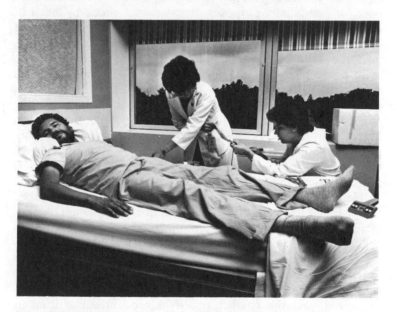

Agent Orange Patient. During the Vietnam War, the military used a defoliant named Agent Orange to clear tree and shrub cover from areas with major enemy activity. Agent Orange may have caused unanticipated medical problems, including cancer, in American soldiers exposed to it. The federal government and other researchers have investigated the question without definitive results, and the state of New Jersey has established an Agent Orange Commission to look into the problems of New Jersey veterans. This photograph, taken at Barnet Hospital, Paterson, in 1986, shows a veteran receiving medical treatment under the commission's auspices. PHOTO BY TONY VELEZ, COURTESY THE PHOTOGRAPHER.

108ONE STATE IN ARMS

in the 1980 presidential election. During the campaign he persuaded the country that the domestic conflict over Vietnam was in the past and that it had been an exception to normal American behavior. The country forgot that there had been serious division over previous wars.

The dawn of the 1990s demonstrated the extent to which popular support for the military had rebounded from the bleakest years of the controversy over Vietnam. After the collapse of communism in Eastern Europe over 1989 and 1990, any number of Americans predicted a "peace dividend" for the nation. That is, the receding Soviet threat would allow cuts in American defense spending, permitting increased financial support for nonmilitary purposes. It came as a shock to much of the public, then, when Iraq invaded the tiny oil sheikdom of Kuwait in August 1990 and conflict loomed as a serious possibility.

Suspense built over the rest of the year. Through the final months of 1990, and the first days of 1991, the United States led a United Nations coalition in a massive build-up to defend Saudi Arabia from any further Iraqi advance (Operation Desert Shield). In January President George Bush secured congressional approval to use military force to expel Iraqi forces from Kuwait. Then, in a lightning campaign called "Desert Storm" (commanded by a former Lawrenceville, New Jersey, resident, General Normal Schwartzkopf), the coalition crushed Iraq's armed forces in mere weeks and liberated Kuwait. American and allied casualties were minimal, the troops performed brilliantly, and America's expensive arsenal of high-technology weaponry seemed to prove its worth in combat. It was an impressive display of military might, and most of the public was thrilled. Opposition to the war was muted and largely disorganized, and the conflict ended before antiwar sentiments became especially coherent. A protracted struggle, with higher allied casualties, certainly would have engendered a more vigorous antiwar response.

As in all other American conflicts, New Jersey played its role in the Persian Gulf War. The Garden State felt the nation's early uneasiness over the looming war, and then shared in the common euphoria as the allies overwhelmed Iraq. Yellow ribbons, the popular sign of support for the troops, appeared on lapels, doorways, office walls, automobiles—almost anywhere the public might see them. On a grimmer note, however, New Jersey hospitals were put on alert to receive thousands of combat casualties (who fortunately never arrived), and families and towns waited for news of loved ones in the Gulf. The news was not only good: Two Navy flyers, Jeffrey Zaun of Cherry Hill and Robert Wentzel of Metuchen, were among the first allied aviators shot down. Taken prisoner, both survived and were eventually set free, but others were not so lucky. Major Marie Rossi of Oradell, an Army helicopter pilot, was one of the 365 Americans killed during the war; she died in a helicopter crash only days after flying missions in direct support of combat operations.

New Jersey maintained its traditional position as a logistics center. McGuire Air Force Base had flights operating to and from the Gulf around the clock, and personnel at the Navy ammunition depot at Earle played a critical role in keeping the fleet armed and combat ready. While state National Guard infantry units saw no action, Guard logistical formations were sent overseas and took an active part in Desert Storm—which was one of the most difficult and successful logistics operations in history. These troops did their jobs well, and their service was another reminder of the extent to which state units had become integral parts of the larger national military machine.

Together with the regular soldiers, sailors, and air crews, the New Jersey Guard personnel also demonstrated something of the effectiveness of America's post-draft, all-volunteer military. Service in the armed forces had come a long way from the colonial militia. Then, at least in theory, military commanders relied on the civil obligation of an armed citizenry to fill the ranks. There was no talk of such an obligation in the Gulf; war was now the business of highly trained professionals. As for the National Guard, its members are part-time professionals, but Desert Shield and Desert Storm left little doubt about their skills.

New Jersey and the Military: A Retrospect

New Jersey's involvement with military affairs has been long and deep. In one form or another, the military has been a fact of life for residents of the Garden State, even if not an intrusive one at times. No longer a battlefield itself after the War for Independence—unless one counts the beach front in 1942 or Newark in 1967—the state sent its sons and daughters to fight on fields all over the world in the following centuries. It has had few equals as a base of training and supply, and its civilian economy has been a critical source of the sinews of war for over two hundred years. New Jersey has also reflected the evolution of the broader themes of American military policy. From fighting small-scale wars with militia and other local forces, the state experimented with volunteers and regular soldiers on the European model, and finally it sent its troops into the mass conscripted battalions of the modern nation-state. Along with these changes, of course, came the effects of technology and industry which made warfare ever more deadly, and in which New Jersey played such a signal role.

The state's experience in arms was also indicative of the growth of the federal system. In the colonial period, and even in the early republic, local militia provided the backbone of American military strength. While New Jersey has retained its own military forces in the form of the National Guard, military policy and action have become the prerogatives of the national government. State militia, volunteer, and guard forces rallied to the colors repeatedly over the years, but they served under federal commanders and pursued federal missions. Governors have called out their local troops for various reasons, fortunately more often for emergency rescues and disaster relief or for ceremonial duties than for riot control or for the suppression of domestic tumult. Federal officials, however, have the last word on the use of state forces and have the authority to muster them in time of need, with or without the permission of a governor. Similarly, state governments have little control over military policy. Opposition from New Jersey Democrats did not stop Lincoln from sending New Jersey men and resources to the front; antiwar protests during the Vietnam years did not stop Presidents Lyndon Johnson and Richard Nixon from doing much the same thing for quite some time. The national military engine is a mighty one indeed.

Yet Johnson and Nixon did not have Lincoln's cause nor, ultimately, his political control. If Vietnam demonstrated something about the limits of America's ability to project its military might overseas, it also said something about waging an undeclared war after losing control of the necessary political machinery. And after Vietnam, things were not the same. Americans, New Jerseyans along with the rest, were less willing to commit their sons and daughters to the fortunes of war without good cause and without a clear sense of mission. Along with a majority of Congress, most of the New Jersey congressional delegation voted for the War Powers Act of 1972, which requires congressional approval after thirty days of any presidential decision to send troops into a foreign war. Moreover, if Americans have come to accept the necessity of maintaining a large military establishment in time of peace, as previous generations never did, the aftermath of Vietnam has made many more citizens aware of the implications of that fact.

Thus, like any engine, the American military machine has occasionally run out of tune. Arguably, however, it has never run completely out of control. Even when undertaking assignments provoking popular opposition, the military has remained subordinate to civilian authority, as provided in the Constitution. Nor has the country defined opposition to a war as treasonous. Protests against conflicts in 1812, Mexico, the Civil War, the Vietnam War, and others have created discord, turmoil, and bitterness; but despite some government attempts to muzzle dissent, most protesters have been able to speak their minds. Even attempted crackdowns on dissent—the Red Scare and the McCarthy investigations come to mind here—ultimately have failed. War and military concerns have sent the nation, and with it the state, down some avenues that, in looking back, it has regretted. But Americans have rallied from low points, and they have managed fairly well the tricky task of maintaining their democratic values while maintaining the military means to defend them.

USS **New Jersey,** *off Beirut, Lebanon. After service in Vietnam, the New Jersey went into mothballs (decommissioned storage) until 1982. Modernized and brought back to the fleet as part of the military build-up under President Ronald Reagan, the battleship patrolled off the coast of Lebanon during the winter of 1983–84. She fired several times in support of U.S. Marines ashore.* U.S. NAVAL INSTITUTE.

GLOSSARY

Entries are in alphabetical order, with page numbers in parentheses showing where the terms first appear in the narrative.

Adjutant General (p. 56): chief administrative officer of New Jersey's military units. The office was established to administer the affairs of the National Guard and to maintain all New Jersey state military records. The adjutant general also serves as a military adviser to the governor.

Artillery (p. 26): large-caliber weapons, generally operated by gun crews rather than by single soldiers. They include cannon, howitzers (small cannon which fire at shorter ranges and higher trajectories than long-range artillery), antiaircraft guns, mortars (cannon that fire shells at very high trajectories to clear obstacles or fortifications and land behind them), and certain rockets.

Axis Powers (p. 83): the alliance of Germany, Italy, Japan, and other powers that opposed the Allies (Great Britain, the Soviet Union, the United States, France, China, and others) in World War II.

Breech-loading rifle (p. 67): a rifle loaded through an opening in the rear (the breech) of the barrel. The opening allowed the feeding of a cartridge into a firing chamber relatively quickly, which was a breechloader's chief advantage over the more cumbersome muzzle-loading weapons. Practical breechloaders were known as early as the Revolutionary War, the invention of British Major Patrick Ferguson. Certain breechloaders (notably the Sharps rifle) saw use during the Civil War, especially in cavalry outfits. But military conservatism and production problems prevented any general issue of breechloading arms to U.S. forces until after the Civil War.

Rifles themselves were employed in the Revolution, but only in selected units. They were impractical for use as the main infantry weapon. A rifled barrel has spiraling grooves, called rifling, on the inside, which put a spin on the bullet as it passes through, increasing its range and accuracy. Early rifles, however, were muzzle-loaded and were not capable of rapid fire. The bullet, which was a lead ball, had to be slightly larger than the bore (the inside of the barrel) to engage

113

the rifling and receive the required spin. The rifleman had to force the ball down the muzzle with brute strength, sometimes actually hammering the ramrod. Firing quickly was out of the question. During the Civil War, the adoption of the minie ball (a conical bullet named for its French inventor, Captain C. E. Minie) allowed the introduction of rifled muzzle-loaders as the standard weapon. The minie ball was smaller than the bore of the weapon. When the rifle was fired, the gases generated by the exploding gunpowder expanded the base of the minie ball so that it engaged the rifling in the barrel. This muzzle-loader was vastly more efficient than the old ones—an "improvement" measured in the ghastly Civil War casualty figures. Breechloaders, by eliminating the need to ram the ammunition down the bore, made loading and firing even faster.

Conscription (p. 48): a draft, or the choosing of soldiers by lot or other selection process from a pool designated as eligible. "Conscripts," or "draftees," are not soldiers who have volunteered for duty; rather, their enlistments have been mandated by a conscription law. American armed forces relied on limited conscription during the Revolutionary and Civil wars, but the first comprehensive draft came during World War I.

Constabulary (p. 14): a police force. Some military forces, such as the early militia or the modern National Guard, assume police functions under certain conditions in the absence of civilian authorities. In several European countries, constabularies are in fact military forces organized separately from the regular army; they are usually concerned with domestic security.

Cruise missile (p. 100): an unmanned aircraft which explodes on impact with a target. Cruise missiles are relatively cheap (as missiles go) and hard to detect because their guidance systems can maneuver them below the effective altitudes of most radar. During the 1970s and 1980s, the United States, other Western nations, and the Soviet Union developed and deployed cruise missiles intensively. These weapons figured prominently in the arms-reduction agreements between President Ronald Reagan and Soviet General Secretary Mikhail Gorbachev.

European model (p. 26): the military system prevalent in Britain and continental Europe during the eighteenth century. European armies relied on long-term enlistments and professionally trained soldiers serving under strict discipline. These troops served in units of standardized sizes within similar command structures, and fought using the linear formations of the era. That is, rival forces faced off in opposing lines of battle—usually two ranks deep—to deliver massed volumes of musket fire.

Fascism (p. 82): an ideology that glorifies the nation-state at the expense of the individual. Its main components are racism, aggressive military policy, autocratic leadership, and opposition to democratic and socialist movements. The term was first used by the party of Benito Mussolini, who ruled Italy from 1922 until the country was defeated in World War II. It has also been applied to other right-wing movements, especially the Nazi regime in Germany.

Flank attack (p. 61): an attack from the side (flank). Flank attacks were especially dangerous in the eighteenth and nineteenth centuries, when linear formations dominated battlefields. When a line (rank) of troops faced forward, it could project all of its fire to the front and almost none to the side. If an attacker could bring its line to bear on an enemy's flank, it could pour its fire into the side of his relatively defenseless ranks. Flank attacks could inflict terrible casualties, because the fire of attacking formations could hardly miss hitting someone as it traveled the length of the enemy ranks. In addition, a successful flank attack generally contained an element of surprise. Usually, a unit could detect a movement near its flank and adjust its defensive positions to forestall the assault. But if it failed to see the threat, the shock of the sudden attack alone could throw it into chaos. Stonewall Jackson's pounce on the Union flank at Chancellorsville, Virginia, in 1863 illustrated what such an attack could do even to a numerous and well-armed enemy.

Frigate (p. 39): in the age of sail, a three-masted warship; most had between thirty and forty guns. Frigates were ships of medium strength, the equivalent of modern destroyers or light cruisers. During the War of 1812, frigates such as *Constitution* and *Constellation* were the pride of the small United States fleet. Today, a frigate is a ship roughly intermediate between a destroyer and a cruiser.

Gatling gun (p. 69): an early machine gun. Named for its inventor, Richard J. Gatling, it was a hand-cranked, rapid-fire weapon with a revolving cluster of barrels. Gatling guns saw duty in the years after the Civil War, but by World War I they had given way to more efficient and deadly single-barreled automatic weapons.

Great Depression (p. 82): a severe economic depression in the 1930s, following the stock market crash of October 1929. Among its causes were overproduction of goods, limited foreign markets, overexpansion of credit, and speculation in the stock market. Many employers cut back their work forces or went out of business. In 1933, at the peak of the Depression, about one-third of the American labor force was out of work.

Impress (p. 31): to forcibly expropriate for military use. In the eighteenth century, most Western governments had legal means of impressing supplies, equipment, and even men for their armed forces. Usually, impressment was a last resort. In 1812, British impressment of sailors from American ships was one of the reasons for the U.S. declaration of war.

Ironclad (p. 43): an armored warship. Although other nations had experimented with partially armored vessels, the first practical ironclad was the Confederacy's CSS *Virginia*. The rebel navy built an armored superstructure on the hull of the old federal wooden steam warship *Merrimac,* which had been scuttled when the Union abandoned Norfolk Navy Yard, Virginia, early in the war. (Many histories still refer to *Virginia* as *Merrimac.*) The Union's *Monitor* was the first man-of-war designed from the beginning as a fully armored ship.

Japanese imperial system (p. 82): The Japanese government, from the late 1920s through World War II, was dominated by the military. The head of the government was the emperor, who was considered divine but had limited actual power. The government, although parliamentary in form, was nationalistic, antiwestern, territorially expansionist, and militaristic. A senior military officer generally served as premier.

Kiloton (p. 96): a measure of the force of an atomic explosion. One kiloton equals a thousand tons of dynamite; a megaton equals a million.

Logistics (p. 8): the procurement, management, maintenance, and transport of military supplies, equipment, facilities, and personnel.

Megaton (p. 96): see *kiloton.*

Men-of-war (p. 58): warships. The term is generally applied only to vessels of a legally recognized navy.

Musket (p. 9): a smooth-barreled infantry weapon, loaded through the muzzle and fired from the shoulder. This was the standard infantry arm from the late seventeenth through the mid-nineteenth century. It was replaced by the rifle (see *breech-loading rifle*) in most Western armies after the 1850s.

Muzzle-loader (p. 67): a weapon loaded through the muzzle. Most small arms (muskets, rifles, and pistols) and cannon manufactured before the middle of the nineteenth century were muzzle-loaders. See *breech-loading rifle.*

Nazi (p. 82): A member of the National Socialist German Workers Party, which was led by Adolf Hitler after 1920. The Nazi regime, which ruled Germany from 1933 to 1945, was totalitarian, antisemitic, anti-Communist, and extremely nationalistic. Its territorial and national ambitions led directly to World War II; its policy of genocide was responsible for the murder of more than 6 million Jews and over 2 million Poles, gypsies and other Europeans.

Nuclear warhead (p. 100): the explosive charge of a nuclear weapon. Warheads travel on a variety of delivery systems, including missiles, bombs, and cannon shells.

Ordnance (p. 67): military equipment and supplies having to do with artillery. The term commonly refers to cannon, other big guns, and ammunition, although it also includes transport and maintenance.

Panzer (p. 85): tank. The word is German for "armor." It entered the world's vocabulary early in World War II as Nazi tank units overran Poland, the Low Countries, and France. *Panzer* also referred to other armored vehicles, such as tank destroyers and self-propelled artillery. The panzers were at the heart of the blitzkrieg (lightning war) tactic, which emphasized speed and mobility, breakthroughs on narrow fronts, and the disruption of enemy command and communication systems. In fact, it was the skilled German use of their panzers that was decisive: when the war began, German tanks were not necessarily superior to Allied ones, but German tactics (that is, the handling of units in combat), leadership, and training outclassed anything they faced on the battlefield.

Privateer (p. 26): a privately owned warship with legal permission from a legitimate government to wage war on that government's behalf. The term also refers to the ship's commander. A privateer is distinct from a pirate, who plunders illegally on his own behalf. Down to the early nineteenth century, governments frequently issued letters of marque (authorization) to private shipowners to sail as privateers to supplement naval strength. At times, privateers cooperated with regular naval forces, but most often they operated alone in raids against enemy commercial shipping. During the Revolution, for example, American privateers inflicted more damage on the British than did the small Continental Navy. Privateers also fought in the War of 1812.

Salvo (p. 58): a simultaneous discharge of two or more guns.

Snafu (p. 70): slang expression for a badly confused situation. The term is of unknown but probably American military origin; it stands for "Situation Normal—All Fouled Up." Rather than "Fouled," troops often used a less genteel "F-word."

Sortie (p. 58): (verb) to attack suddenly from a defensive position; also (noun) such an attack. At Yorktown, for example, in 1781, the beleaguered British launched a sortie against the Americans and French in an unsuccessful effort to break their siege. *Sortie* has also come to mean a single mission by a single aircraft. If an aircraft carrier launches ten sorties, for instance, it sends out ten airplanes.

U-boat (p. 83): a submarine; German for *unterseeboot*. The first practical military submarine was the invention of John Holland, whose team did much of its development work in New Jersey. The Germans, however, first demonstrated the submarine's effectiveness in warfare. In World Wars I and II, U-boats almost severed the vital Atlantic shipping lanes between the U.S. and Europe. In the Pacific, American submarines proved even more deadly against Japanese shipping. By 1945, U.S. subs had virtually wiped out the major ships of the Japanese merchant marine and had contributed significantly to the elimination of the Imperial Navy as an effective fighting force.

NOTES

Full citations are found in "Sources," p. 120.

Chapter One

1. Smith, *The History of the Colony of Nova Caesaria,* 64.
2. Ibid., 518.
3. Johnson, *Swedish Settlements on the Delaware,* 1:377.
4. Purvis, "The Aftermath of Fort William Henry's Fall," 69.

Chapter Two

1. Lender and Martin, *Citizen Soldier,* 145.

Chapter Three

1. Quoted in Raum, *The History of New Jersey,* 391.
2. Quoted in Leckie, *The Wars of America,* 1:256–57.
3. Quoted in Herrmann, "Charles Creighton Stratton," 118.

Chapter Four

1. Millis, *Arms and Men,* 102.
2. Quoted in Siegel, *For the Glory of the Union,* 17.
3. *Newark Daily Advertiser,* 5 April 1861, p. 1.
4. Schwartz, "Rodman M. Price," 124–25.
5. Quoted in Simpson, "Chaplain John C. Lenhart," 13.
6. Quoted in ibid., 10.
7. Lincoln, "Missing in Action," part 1, p. 54.
8. Ibid.
9. Ibid.
10. Robertson, *The Civil War Letters of General Robert McAllister,* 608.

Chapter Six

1. Schonbach, *Radicals and Visionaries,* 68.
2. Morison, *The Two-Ocean War,* 109.
3. Cunningham, *New Jersey: America's Main Road,* 297.

Chapter Seven

1. McCormick, *Rutgers: A Bicentennial History,* 277.
2. Bogue, *The Population of the United States,* 9.

SOURCES

Introduction

James Axtell, *The Invasion Within: The Conflict of Cultures in Colonial North America* (New York, 1985)

Richard P. McCormick, *New Jersey: From Colony to State* (1964; reprint, Newark: New Jersey Historical Society, 1981)

Allan R. Millet and Peter Maslowski, *For the Common Defense: A Military History of the United States of America* (New York, 1984)

Walter Millis, *Arms and Men: A Study of American Military History* (New York, 1956)

Samuel Smith, *The History of the Colony of Nova Caesaria, or New Jersey . . .* (Burlington, N.J., 1765).

Chapter One

John Warner Barber and Henry Howe, *Historical Collections of the State of New Jersey* (New York, 1844)

John E. Ferling, *A Wilderness of Miseries: War and Warriors in Early America* (Westport, Conn., 1980)

Edgar Jacob Fisher, *New Jersey as a Royal Province, 1738 to 1776* (New York, 1911)

Amandus Johnson, *Swedish Settlements on the Delaware* (New York, 1911), Vol. 1

Herbert C. Kraft, *The Lenape: Archaeology, History, and Ethnography* (Newark, 1987)

Douglas Edward Leach, *Arms for Empire: A Military History of the British Colonies in North America, 1607–1763* (New York, 1963)

Francis Bazley Lee, ed., *New Jersey as a Colony and as a State* (New York, 1902), Vol. 1

McCormick, *New Jersey: From Colony to State*

Earl Schenck Miers, ed., *The Story of New Jersey* (New York, 1945), Vol. 1

Isaac S. Mumford, *Civil and Political History of New Jersey* (Camden, 1848)

National Park Service, Delaware Water Gap National Recreation Area, "The Van Campen Inn" Brochure (1984)

New Jersey, *Votes and Proceedings of the General Assembly of the Province of New Jersey* (Burlington, N.J., 1765)

Archives of the State of New Jersey, 2nd ser., 35 vols. (Newark, 1880–1949)

Thomas L. Purvis, "The Aftermath of Fort William Henry's Fall: New Jersey Captives Among the French and Indians," New Jersey History 103, 3–4 (Fall/Winter 1985): 69–80

John O. Raum, *The History of New Jersey,* (Philadelphia, 1877) Vol. 1

Smith, *Colony of Nova Caesaria*

Paul A. Stellhorn and Michael J. Birkner, *The Governors of New Jersey, 1664–1974: Biographical Essays* (Trenton, 1982)

Charles A. Weslager, *The English on the Delaware: 1610–1682* (New Brunswick, 1967)

Carl R. Woodward, *Ploughs and Politicks: Charles Read of New Jersey and His Notes on Agriculture, 1714–1774* (New Brunswick, 1941)

Chapter Two

Barber and Howe, *Historical Collections*

Joseph J. Casino, "Elizabethtown 1782: The Prisoners-of-War Negotiations and the Pawns of War," *New Jersey History,* 102, 1–2 (Spring–Summer 1984): 1–35

Linda Grant De Pauw, "Women in Combat: The Revolutionary War Experience," *Armed Forces and Society,* 7 (1981): 209–26

Douglas Southall Freeman, *George Washington: A Biography* (New York, 1951–52), Vols. 4, 5

Adrian C. Leiby, *The Revolutionary War in the Hackensack Valley: The Jersey Dutch and the Neutral Ground, 1775–1783,* 2nd ed., (New Brunswick, 1980)

Mark Edward Lender, *The New Jersey Soldier,* (Trenton, 1975)

Mark E. Lender, "The Social Structure of the New Jersey Brigade," in *The Military in America: From the Colonial Era to the Present,* ed. Peter Karsten (New York, 1980), 27–44

Mark E. Lender and James Kirby Martin, *Citizen Soldier: The Revolutionary War Journal of Joseph Bloomfield* (Newark, 1982)

Jared C. Lobdell, "Six Generals Gather Forage: the Engagement at Quibbletown, 1777," *New Jersey History,* 102, 3–4 (Fall–Winter 1984): 35–49

Leonard Lundin, *Cockpit of the Revolution: The War of Independence in New Jersey* (Princeton, 1940)

McCormick, *New Jersey: From Colony to State*

James Kirby Martin and Mark Edward Lender, *A Respectable Army: The Military Origins of the Republic, 1763–1789* (Arlington Heights, Ill., 1982)

Millet and Maslowski, *For the Common Defense*

Millis, *Arms and Men*

Samuel Stelle Smith, *The Battle of Trenton* (Monmouth Beach, N.J., 1965)

Samuel Stelle Smith, *Winter at Morristown, 1779–1780: The Darkest Hour* (Monmouth Beach, N.J., 1979)
George Washington, *The Writings of George Washington from the Original Manuscript Sources, 1745–1799,* ed. John C. Fitzpatrick, (Washington, D.C., 1931–44).

Chapter Three

Marcus Cunliffe, *Soldiers and Civilians: The Martial Spirit in America, 1775–1865* (Boston, 1968)
Albert Gleaves, *James Lawrence, Captain, United States Navy, Commander of the Chesapeake* (New York, 1904)
Frederick M. Hermann, "Charles Creighton Stratton," in Stellhorn and Birkner, *Governors of New Jersey,* 117–119
Alfred M. Hester, *South Jersey: A History, 1664–1924* (New York, 1924), Vol. 1
Richard H. Kohn, *Eagle and Sword: The Federalists and the Creation of the Military Establishment in America, 1783–1802* (New York, 1975)
Irving Kull, ed., *New Jersey: A History* (New York, 1930), Vol. 1
Robert Leckie, *The Wars of America* (New York, 1968), Vol. 1
Lee, *New Jersey as a Colony and as a State,* Vol. 2
David F. Long, *Ready to Hazard: A Biography of Commodore William Bainbridge* (Durham, N.H., 1981)
Samuel Marsh, Military Pension Application with supporting documents, 18 May 1819, Pension Claim No. 36065, National Archives, Washington, D.C.
Millet and Maslowski, *For the Common Defense*
Millis, *Arms and Men*
Rudolph J. Pasler and Margaret C. Pasler, *The New Jersey Federalists* (Rutherford, N.J., 1975)
Hugh F. Pullen, *The Shannon and the Chesapeake* (Toronto, Ont., 1986)
Harvey Strum, "New Jersey Politics and the War of 1812," *New Jersey History* 105 (Fall/Winter 1987): 37–69
John U. Terrell, *Zebulon M. Pike: The Life and Times of an Adventurer* (New York, 1986)
Russell F. Weigley, *Towards an American Army: Military Thought from Washington to Marshall* (New York, 1962).

Chapter Four

Cunliffe, *Soldiers and Civilians*
John Y. Foster, *New Jersey and the Rebellion* (Newark, 1868)
J. F. C. Fuller, *The Conduct of War, 1789–1961* (New Brunswick, 1961)
Robert Underwood Johnson and Clarence Clough Buel, eds., *Battles and Leaders of the Civil War,* 4 vols. (New York, 1887)
Charles M. Knapp, *New Jersey Politics During the Period of the Civil War and Reconstruction* (Geneva, N.Y., 1924)

Leckie, *Wars of America*

Edwin Lincoln, "Missing in Action: The Civil War Letters of Alfred Lyman Lincoln," *New Jersey History* 106:3–4 (Fall/Winter 1988), pp. 53–77

Robert McCallister, *The Civil War Letters of General Robert McAllister*, ed. James I. Robertson, Jr. (New Brunswick, 1965)

James M. McPherson, *Battle Cry of Freedom: The Civil War Era* (New York, 1988)

Millet and Maslowski, *For the Common Defense*

Millis, *Arms and Men*

Miers, *Story of New Jersey*, Vol. 2

Newark Daily Advertiser, 5 April 1861

Henry R. Pyne, *Ride to War: The History of the First New Jersey Cavalry*, ed. Earl Schenck Miers (New Brunswick, 1961)

Raum, *History of New Jersey*, Vol. 2

Joel Schwartz, "Rodman M. Price," in Stellhorn and Birkner, *Governors of New Jersey*, 121–26

Alan A. Siegel, *For the Glory of the Union: Myth, Reality, and the Media in Civil War New Jersey* (Rutherford, N.J., 1984)

Drew Simpson, "Chaplain John C. Lenhart," unpublished MS, 1985

Maurice Tandler, "The Political Front in Civil War New Jersey," *Proceedings of the New Jersey Historical Society* 83 (1965): 223–33

Weigley, *Towards an American Army*

William C. Wright, "New Jersey's Military Role in the Civil War Reconsidered," New Jersey History 92, 4 (Winter 1974): 197–210

James S. Yard, "Joel Parker: The War Governor of New Jersey," *Proceedings of the New Jersey Historical Society* 10 (1888–89): 57–92.

Chapter Five

Vincent J. Esposito, *The West Point Atlas of American Wars*, 2 vols. (New York, 1959), Vol. 2

Frank Freidel, *The Splendid Little War* (Boston, 1958)

Hester, *South Jersey*, Vol. 1

Kull, *New Jersey: A History*, Vol. 2

Leckie, *Wars of America*, Vol. 2

D. McNally, comp., *Soldiers and Sailors of New Jersey in the Spanish-American War* (Newark, 1898)

Millet and Maslowski, *For the Common Defense*

Millis, *Arms and Men*

William Nelson, ed., *The New Jersey Coast in Three Centuries*, 2 vols. (New York, 1902)

Stellhorn and Birkner, *Governors of New Jersey*

Chapter Six

Hanson W. Baldwin, *World War I* (New York, 1962)

John T. Cunningham, *New Jersey: America's Main Road,* rev. ed. (Andover, N.J., 1976)

Susan Doan-Johnson, "Exhibition Showcases NJ Women at Work," *Trenton Times,* 15 March 1987

Esposito, *West Point Atlas,* Vol. 2

Federal Writers Project, *The WPA Guide to the 1930s: New Jersey* (1939; reprinted, New Brunswick, 1986)

Susan H. Godson, "Capt. Joy Bright Hancock and the Role of Women in the US Navy," *New Jersey History* 105, 1–2 (Spring/Summer 1987): 1–18

Hester, *South Jersey,* Vol. 1

Theodore R. Jamison, "Joyce Kilmer, Soldier-Poet: A Centenary Perspective," *New Jersey History* 105, 1–2 (Spring/Summer 1987): 19–40

James Jandrowitz, " 'This Is Not a Drill': An Oral History of Three Pearl Harbor Veterans," *New Jersey History* 106, 1–2 (Spring/ Summer 1988), 41–59

Leckie, *Wars of America,* Vol. 2

Richard P. McCormick, *Rutgers: A Bicentennial History* (New Brunswick, 1966)

Millet and Maslowski, *For the Common Defense*

Millis, *Arms and Men*

Samuel Eliot Morison, *The Two-Ocean War: A Short History of the United States Navy in the Second World War* (Boston, 1963)

Bernard C. Nalty, *Strength for the Fight: A History of Black Americans in the Military* (New York, 1986)

New Jersey History Committee, *Outline History of New Jersey* (New Brunswick, 1950)

E. B. Potter, *Bull Halsey* (Annapolis, Md., 1985)

Donald A. Raichle, *From A Normal Beginning: The Origins of Kean College of New Jersey* (Rutherford, N.J., 1980)

Morris Schonbach, *Radicals and Visionaries: A History of Dissent in New Jersey,* New Jersey Historical Series, 12 (Princeton, 1964)

Jones Richard Seeley, *A History of the American Legion* (Indianapolis, Ind., 1946)

Laurence Stallings, *The Doughboys* (New York, 1963)

Stellhorn and Birkner, *Governors of New Jersey*

Paul Stillwell, *Battleship New Jersey: An Illustrated History* (Annapolis, Md., 1986)

Studs Terkel, *"The Good War": An Oral History of World War Two* (New York, 1984)

"USS Atlanta," Permanent Exhibit, Atlanta Historical Society, Atlanta, Ga.

John D. Venable, *Out of the Shadow: The Story of Charles Edison* (East Orange, N.J., 1978)

Chapter Seven

Stephen E. Ambrose, *Rise to Globalism: American Foreign Policy, 1938–1976,* Pelican History of the United States, 8, rev. ed. (New York, 1976)

Donald J. Bogue, *The Population of the United States* (New York, 1959)

Cunningham, *New Jersey: America's Main Road*

McCormick, *Rutgers: A Bicentennial History*

Millet and Maslowski, *For the Common Defense*

Millis, *Arms and Men*

Newark Evening News Morgue Collection, Newark Public Library, Newark, N.J.

David M. Oshinsky, "Fort Monmouth and McCarthy: The Victims Remember," *New Jersey History* 100, 1–2 (Spring/Summer 1982): 1–14

Raichle, *From A Normal Beginning*

"Repeal the New G.I. Bill?" *New Jersey Military Education Advisory Council Bulletin,* N.J. Dept. of Higher Education (March 1986), 1

"Scars from '67 Riots in Newark Are Still Visible in Central Ward," *New York Times,* 13 July 1987, Sec. B, p. 1

Stellhorn and Birkner, *Governors of New Jersey*

Stillwell, *Battleship New Jersey*

SUGGESTIONS FOR FURTHER READING

Full bibliographic citations are given in this section only for titles not listed elsewhere. All other titles are fully cited in *Sources,* p. 120.

I have held endnotes to a minimum. Only direct quotations have received formal notes; the sources most helpful in writing the book are listed by chapter in *Sources,* p. 120. Readers can pursue individual subjects in greater depth by consulting the works listed there. The following bibliographical essay describes many of them and also introduces some of the most useful of the other titles on the military in New Jersey.

With few exceptions, authors have paid little attention to military affairs in the Garden State after the War for American Independence. In fact, there is no comprehensive history of the issue at the state level, and with few exceptions the student will find martial subjects treated almost on a war-by-war basis. Details are scattered throughout many studies, which often touch on only a few facets of the broader issue. Thus the student would do well to establish a historical framework to deal with the partial views available in the New Jersey literature. Among the best general works on American military history are Walter Millis's *Arms and Men* and Allan R. Millet and Peter Maslowski's *For the Common Defense.* The Millis book is a classic; historians point to it as one of the initial and most important contributions to the "new military history," which has emphasized the social, economic, and political implications of military affairs rather than taking a "guns and battles" approach to the subject. I relied extensively on both of these volumes in interpreting my material.

A major study of New Jersey in the colonial wars is long overdue. Vital information on early military activities and operations is available in Samuel Smith, *The History of the Colony of Nova Caesaria,* which has some especially revealing passages on European clashes with the Lenape, and John Warner Barber and Henry Howe, *Historical Collections of the State of New Jersey,* an invaluable source of early New Jerseyana. Over the years, several general histories of the state added considerable detail on colonial military operations involving New Jersey, and the following are still worth consulting: John O. Raum, *The History of New Jersey,* vol. 1; Francis Bazley Lee, ed., *New Jersey as a Colony and as a State;* Edgar Jacob Fisher, *New Jersey as a Royal Province;* and Earl Schenck Miers, ed., *The Story of New Jersey.* On occasion, more recent scholarship has taken advantage of newly discovered documentary evidence on the earlier period. Thomas L. Purvis, for example, in "The Aftermath of Fort William Henry's Fall," has demonstrated that a good historian can use this new evidence to shed quite a bit of light on the provincial military. On the whole, however, we have only a woefully incomplete view of the nature and extent of the colony's participation in the campaigns against the French and Indians, and an even cloudier view of the functioning of the local militia down to the 1760s.

The case is different for the Revolutionary War. New Jersey's position as an active theater of operations has attracted considerable scholarly attention, and much of the resulting work on the armed struggle in the state has been substantial. Leonard Lundin's *Cockpit of the Revolution* is still one of the most comprehensive works, although it could now stand revision in the light of two generations of subsequent scholarship. The major actions of the war have also generated a number of fine books, some of the best being William Scudder Stryker, *The Battle of Monmouth* (Princeton, 1927); Thomas Fleming, *The Forgotten Victory: The Battle for New Jersey—1780* (New York, 1973); Samuel Stelle Smith, *Winter at Morristown;* and William M. Dwyer, *The Day Is Ours! November, 1776–January, 1777: An Inside View of the Battles of Trenton and Princeton* (New York, 1983).

The fighting in New Jersey has also produced some interesting social histories. One of the best studies of a locality caught in the cross currents of war is Adrian C. Leiby's *Revolutionary War in the Hackensack Valley.* Leiby looks at the war as it affected Jersey Dutch society, where long-standing religious disputes often determined who turned rebel and who stood by the king. Mark Edward Lender has looked at the troops of the state in *The New Jersey Soldier* and in "The Social Structure of the New Jersey Brigade." John Todd White, in "The Truth About Molly Pitcher," pp. 99–105 in James Kirby Martin and Karen R. Stubaus, eds., *The American Revolution: Whose Revolution?* (Huntington, N.Y., 1977), offers a view of women traveling with the American army; the same subject receives deeper treatment in Linda Grant DePauw, "Women in Combat." DePauw's article also draws on the events at the Battle of Monmouth in providing one of the most important perspectives we have on the relationships of women to the revolutionary military. The tories receive their due in Paul H. Smith, "New Jersey Loyalists and the British 'Provincial' Corps in the War for Independence," *New Jersey History* 87, 2 (Summer 1969), 69–78. Considerable New Jersey material is also in James Kirby Martin and Mark Edward Lender, *A Respectable Army.*

There are several good reference volumes on the period. David C. Munn, *Battles and Skirmishes of the American Revolution in New Jersey* (Trenton, 1976), is a useful compilation of land and naval engagements which vividly conveys how constant and costly the military struggle was in the Garden State. Howard K. Peckham, ed., *The Toll of Independence: Engagements and Battle Casualties of the American Revolution* (Chicago, 1974), is less complete for New Jersey than Munn's work, but it has valuable summary tabulations that put New Jersey data in the context of the wider war. Another massive compilation, by the state Adjutant General William Scudder Stryker, is the *Official Register of the Officers and Men of New Jersey in the Revolutionary War* (Trenton, 1872). It is the starting place for unit information and occasional service detail on thousands of soldiers and sailors with the militia and Continental forces; it also provides an overview of New Jersey recruiting laws.

After the Revolutionary period, military history presents lean pickings in New Jersey. This is not surprising, since military historians have traditionally focused on events in the field, and there has been no major battle in New Jersey since the one at Springfield in 1780. Still, students of the Garden State will find much interest in scholarship (most of it less than twenty years old) not concerned primarily with New Jersey. Richard H. Kohn, in *Eagle and Sword,* used some New Jersey material— especially in discussing the "Quasi-War" with France during the late 1790s—while offering a key interpretation of the political battles that surrounded the establishment of the regular American army. The War of 1812 gets some attention in chapters four and five of Lee's *New Jersey as a Colony and as a State,* Vol. 2; and a recent article by Harvey Strum, "New Jersey Politics and the War of 1812," has ably explored the state political controversies that arose from that war. There are several biographies of Jerseymen who fought in 1812, and I found the following particularly useful in tracing the roles of New Jersey personnel and military units: Albert Gleaves, *James Lawrence;* Hugh F. Pullen, *The Shannon and the Chesapeake;* David F. Long, *Ready to Hazard;* and John U. Terrell, *Zebulon M. Pike.*

The impact of democratization and the Industrial Revolution on the conduct of war is a central theme of this volume. Most of the New Jersey literature that treats military matters over the rest of the nineteenth century, however, does not deal directly with this issue. One has to put the pieces together from social and economic history, although a number of excellent unit histories and soldiers' accounts from the Civil War convey a sense of how radically war had changed by the 1860s. I relied on works that were not only very revealing but exciting and often poignant: Henry R. Pyne, *Ride to War;* Robert McAllister's *Civil War Letters;* and Edwin Lincoln, "Missing in Action." Scholars can locate additional diaries and journals in C. E. Dornbusch, comp., *Regimental Publications & Personal Narratives of the Civil War: A Checklist,* Vol. 1, part 4, "New Jersey and Pennsylvania" (New York, 1962).

Information on New Jersey troops and military organizations, as well as recruiting operations, is available in John Y. Foster, *New Jersey and the Rebellion;* William S. Stryker, comp., *Record of Officers and Men of New Jersey in the Civil War, 1861–1865* (Trenton, 1876); and William C. Wright, "New Jersey's Military Role in the Civil War Reconsidered." Civil War politics in New Jersey have attracted more scholarly attention than most other aspects of the struggle. I used the following sources most frequently: James S. Yard, "Joel Parker"; Charles M. Knapp, *New Jersey Politics during the Period of the Civil War and Reconstruction;* Maurice Tandler, "The Political Front in Civil War New Jersey." There is no comprehensive modern study, however, of New Jersey's Civil War experience, and the state's roles as a home front area and as a military-industrial base offer many especially promising opportunities for further study. Those contemplating any such efforts would do well to start by consulting Donald A. Sinclair, *A Bibliography: The Civil War and New Jersey* (New Brunswick, 1968).

Between the Civil War and World War II there is only a scattered literature, and little of it discusses the military implications of new technologies or of New Jersey's political picture. In writing about the Spanish-American War and World War I, I found useful sections or chapters in B. McNally, comp., *Soldiers and Sailors of New Jersey in the Spanish-American War;* William Nelson, ed., *The New Jersey Coast in Three Centuries;* Alfred M. Hester, *South Jersey,* Vol. 1; and Irving Kull, ed., *New Jersey: A History,* Vol. 2. I dug more out of the New Jersey History Committee's *Outline History of New Jersey* and Paul A. Stellhorn and Michael J. Birkner, eds., *The Governors of New Jersey.* Both of these works have important material buried in essays and topical outlines, and both also deal with war as a catalyst for social and economic change. So does Morris Schonbach's *Radicals and Visionaries,* which I used in discussing the Red Scare and the German-American Bund. Still, we could use specific studies of several topics. One is the state National Guard, particularly as it incorporated New Jersey's growing immigrant population of the late nineteenth and early twentieth centuries. Another is the role of martial considerations in the growth of the regional industrial and economic base. Much also needs to be done on the ways state and local authorities have dealt with such issues as the draft, civil liberties and dissent during war, the expansion of federal military facilities, and the broader social and political impact of war and other military activities. One finds only bits and pieces of these stories in the sources cited here.

The picture is somewhat clearer on World War II and its aftermath, if only because John T. Cunningham, in *New Jersey: America's Main Road,* has provided an overview within a wider context. Cunningham deals mostly with the scientific, industrial, and social effects of the conflict on the state, but he also briefly surveys the participation of New Jersey service personnel. There is an interesting tale to pursue in the seashore blackout controversy of 1942. I relied on Samuel Eliot Morison, *The Two-Ocean War,* although there is much more to say on this subject. Richard P. McCormick, *Rutgers: A Bicentennial History,* and Donald A. Raichle, *From A Normal Beginning,* discuss the impact of the war and of postwar readjustments on higher education. Both agree that the GI Bill made a historic contribution in giving the public greater access to college education. We await, however, studies of the influence the war years exerted on the opening of New Jersey society to women and minorities. I have based my discussion on materials in Roger W. Tucker, preparer, *The New Jersey Negro in World War II, Contributions and Activities* (Trenton, 1945); Studs Terkel, *"The Good War";* Bernard C. Nalty, *Strength for the Fight;* and Susan H. Godson, "Capt. Joy Bright Hancock and the Role of Women in the U.S. Navy."

Biographies of individual New Jersey–born soldiers, sailors, war leaders, and in one worthy case, a ship, proved valuable sources as well. I profited especially from John E. Venable, *Out of the Shadow;* E. B. Potter, *Bull Halsey;* Paul Stillwell, *Battleship New Jersey;* and James Jandrowitz, " 'This Is Not a Drill.' " The Jandrowitz article is an example of the important potential for oral history inherent in New Jersey's World War II experience. Postwar affairs have much the same promise, as illustrated in David M. Oshinsky, "Fort Monmouth and McCarthy."

The Vietnam era has generated virtually no military scholarship on New Jersey. There are, of course, plenty of reports by journalists on the use of the National Guard in Newark and other cities in 1967, as well as stories on New Jersey personnel in Southeast Asia and reactions to the war back home. I relied most heavily on the *Newark Evening News* Morgue Collection, Newark Public Library, Newark, NJ, the files of which offer excellent coverage of Vietnam-related subjects until the early 1970s.